# TRACING BIRTHS, DEATHS AND MARRIAGES AT SEA

by Christopher T and Michael J Watts

SOCIETY OF GENEALOGISTS ENTERPRISES LTD

Published by
**Society of Genealogists Enterprises Limited**
14 Charterhouse Buildings
Goswell Road
London EC1M 7BA

ISBN 1 903462 82 7

British Library Cataloguing in Publication Data
A CIP Catalogue record for this book is available from the British Library

## About the Authors

Christopher and Michael Watts are family historians with over thirty years' experience. Both are well-known in the family history world, having been active in, and serving on committees of, Family History Societies.

Chris originally trained and worked as a research chemist but then, for over two decades, worked as an analyst in the defence electronics industry; since 1997 he has been a part-time Reader Adviser at The National Archives. Michael worked as a nuclear engineer and as a lecturer in mechanical engineering at the University of Manchester.

Both took the opportunity of early retirement and have been continuing their studies both for themselves and, on a professional basis, for others. They are well known, especially in the world of family history, for their books and articles, and lectures in the UK, USA, Australia and New Zealand. They have written, or contributed to, several books including *My Ancestor was in the British Army* and *Records of Merchant Shipping and Seamen*. Their book *My Ancestor was a Merchant Seaman*, which was recently fully revised, has been in print for nearly eighteen years and has become recognised as the authoritative work on the subject for both academic and family historians.

Society of Genealogists Enterprises Limited is a wholly owned subsidiary of Society of Genealogists, a registered charity, no 233701

# CONTENTS

# FIGURES

# ACKNOWLEDGEMENTS

The authors wish to express their gratitude to all the custodians of the records described in this book for their assistance in answering questions about the scope, nature and accessibility of their holdings. Particular mention must be made of:

- colleagues at The National Archives, especially: Amanda Bevan, John Carr, Roger Kershaw and Bruno Pappalardo;
- staff at the various General Register Offices, in particular Austin Hayes (England and Wales) and Helen Borthwick (Scotland).
- Neil Staples at the Registry of Shipping and Seamen;
- staff at the Society of Genealogists, especially: Else Churchill, David Walsh and Rosie Miller;
- staff at the National Maritime Museum, especially: Kiri Ross-Jones and Liza Verity.

We are grateful to Colin Chapman for checking the information on marriages by Royal Navy captains, to Sue McBeth and Heather Garnsey, for their assistance with information about registration records in Australia, and to Martin Hadis for information about Argentinean passenger lists.

We also wish to thank the many individuals who have drawn our attention to particular records or provided information about them. Enquiries received by post, by e-mail, from internet groups, from our own and our professional research and from queries posed at the enquiry desks at The National Archives (TNA) at Kew have all contributed in their way. The names of many of these individuals are unknown to us, so it would be invidious to try to name those whom we do know thereby ignoring those whom we do not. To all of them we are grateful.

We are grateful to Marjorie Moore for reading the draft and offering valuable suggestions for improvement and to Sue Lumas for editorial improvements.

Transcripts and facsimiles of Crown copyright records in The National Archives of the UK appear by permission of the Controller of HM Stationery Office. Permission to reuse portions of text and illustrations generated whilst in the employ of TNA, and hence Crown copyright, is acknowledged. Copies of Crown copyright records preserved in the National Maritime Museum, London are published with their permission. The permission of the Guildhall Library, Corporation of London to reproduce an item in their custody from the Bishop of London's Registry is gratefully acknowledged. The copy of an entry in the Marine Register of Births for England appears with the authority of the Registrar General. The copy of the first entry in the Marine Register of Deaths for Scotland is Crown copyright and is reproduced with the permission of the General Register Office for Scotland. We are also grateful to Syd Norris for permission to include a transcript of Martha Louisa Carter's death certificate which he is most fortunate to own.

In a work of this nature, where little has previously appeared in print, it is inevitable that the authors will have overlooked something relevant or misinterpreted some complex legislation or regulations. If so the authors would be grateful to hear of any such oversights or errors so that they may be corrected in any future edition.

# ABBREVIATIONS

The following abbreviations are used throughout the text:

GRO    General Register/Registry Office. The term GRO is used throughout this book to describe the several Registrars-General of Births, Deaths and Marriages to avoid confusion with the Registrar-General of Shipping and Seaman (RGSS).

GROS    General Register Office for Scotland.

NAMR    This refers to the classification of record series used by N A M Rodger in Appendix II of *Naval Records for Genealogists*, (PRO Handbook No 22) 2nd edn. 1988.

MHA    Maritime History Archive, Memorial University of Newfoundland.

NMM    National Maritime Museum.

OIOC    Oriental and India Office Collections of the British Library.

ON    Ship's Official Number

PRO    Public Record Office, now part of, the National Archives of the UK.

PROCAT    The on-line catalogue to the Public Record Office's holdings at the National Archives, available at www.nationalarchives.gov.uk

RGSS    Registrar-General of Shipping and Seamen.

RSS    Registry of Shipping and Seamen (the successor of the RGSS).

TNA    The National Archives of the United Kingdom – probably still better known to researchers as the PRO.

## Some warnings!

When describing records we have tried always to name the repository where the originals are held. If we have inadvertently overlooked this then in the majority of cases it will be in the Public Record Office's holdings at the National Archives (TNA).

Where records have been described as in the process of transfer to TNA, or other repository, then it is essential to enquire before making a visit since the transfer process may take some considerable time during which the material will be unavailable for research.

Some material (in particular at TNA and the NMM) may be outhoused so, unless you are sure, enquire before you make a special visit.

The Registrar-General of Shipping and Seamen kept on changing his mind as to how to arrange material where the surname began with Mc. In some record series they will be found under the letter M; in others under the letter following the Mc prefix (for example McDonald under D). So be prepared to check both.

When looking at Royal Navy records it should be remembered that not everything preceded by HMS actually floated! That description was used for both RN ships and shore stations – the latter were known colloquially as stone or concrete frigates. To distinguish between these consult one of the reference works.[1]

# TERMINOLOGY

Throughout the text we have used the following terms, hopefully consistently:

*Primary source*: A record compiled at the time the event occurred. An example would be a log book entry made by the master of the vessel on which a death occurred. This may be a facsimile, such as a photocopy or microfilm, of an original record.

*Secondary source*: A record compiled subsequent to the event, from primary sources, which interprets what happened. These may themselves be original records: for example the registers compiled by the Registrar-General of Shipping and Seamen. They could also be more modern commentaries (such as a book) or transcripts made from original records.

*Subsidiary source*: A source that incidentally refers to the event. Examples would be the will of a seaman (this would be a subsidiary source related to his death); the baptismal entry of a child born at sea (subsidiary to its birth).

*Seamen:* Most of the Acts and regulations differentiate between masters, seamen and indentured apprentices. As the latter two categories are normally treated similarly we have used the term 'seamen' here to include indentured apprentices but to exclude masters who were normally treated differently.

# INTRODUCTION

Many family historians face the problem of trying to find details of the birth, death or marriage of one of their ancestors that is alleged to have taken place at sea. Some hopefully expect to find that there is a single coherent source recording such events for all British citizens; regrettably this is not the case. As this book will explain the available sources depend more on the nationality of the vessel on which the event took place than on the nationality of the individuals involved. A secondary factor is the destination or port of departure of the vessel. Finally it is significant as to whether the event took place on a merchant vessel or on a ship of the Royal Navy. And if the event relates to a Briton working, or travelling, on a foreign vessel then any record of it becomes even more difficult to trace.

To add further confusion to the mind of the potential researcher are the myths that have grown up about the recording of events at sea. Most of these do not hold up to detailed scrutiny. For instance, although some baptisms at sea from 1893 onwards are recorded in the registers of that church,[2] it is not true that all baptisms at sea were recorded at St. Dunstan, Stepney.[*] An interesting discussion as to how this belief, amongst others, may have arisen is given in an article by Anthony Camp.[3] Masters of merchant vessels, it is also popularly believed, may perform marriage ceremonies; whilst this may perhaps be true for captains of Royal Navy vessels, we have yet to see any convincing evidence for such authority being vested in the masters of merchant vessels.

In this book we will concentrate not so much on such myths, and legal niceties, but rather upon the more practical aspects of just what records of such events have survived, what they might reveal and where to find them. Firstly we will examine the legislation and administrative procedures that govern the recording and

---

[*] In 1957 the then London County Record Office and the RGSS made a sample comparison of the records (*see* BT 167/151 p.35). In 1893 one baptism at sea was recorded in the St. Dunstan registers, but no corresponding birth at sea could be found amongst the 69 births of British children and 169 of other nationalities on British-registered vessels. Of the six baptisms at sea recorded in 1921, in the registers for St. Dunstan, three were from the same family so probably at least two of them were not infants; only two of these six births could be traced amongst over 100 children recorded as born at sea that year.

registration of such events. Do not be put off by this chapter, we will only consider the topic to a depth sufficient to allow you to decide where to look and to understand why the events that you seek should, or should not, be found there. Then we will examine each of the sets of records that resulted, what they contain and where they are to be found. And lastly we will provide practical search strategies to help you conduct your own searches with, hopefully, the minimum of frustration.

# LEGISLATION AND REGULATIONS

## Introduction

The very topic of this chapter may suggest that it can be skipped or left to be read later – please do set aside that urge and read on! In deciding what records are available to assist your research you will need to know three things: what records exist, what time period they cover and what categories of event and/or person they include. The first two can normally be deduced from simple lists derived from examining the records themselves – and these are what you will find in most guides to records. What is rarely given, and what can usually only be determined by looking at the legislation and associated regulations under which they were produced, are what categories of event and/or person are covered. This information is essential if you are not to waste your valuable research time. It is for instance pointless to search a set of records that covers only British citizens if the target of your research is German. Similarly, when searching for a birth on a US-registered ship leaving the UK, you might ignore records that you thought only applied to British-registered ships unless you realised that for some periods of time they also cover non-British registered passenger ships with a port of departure or destination in the United Kingdom.

In this chapter we will look, as concisely as possible, at the UK legislation that covers the recording of births, deaths and marriages at sea. In addition we will examine the regulations issued to the masters of merchant ships and to Royal Navy officers that instructed them in how to comply with the legislation. It is these regulations that interpreted, sometimes incorrectly or inconsistently, the legislative requirements into practical procedures. From this will come an understanding of what records were created, over what period, and what they should have covered. Later chapters will examine the survival of these records and their detailed contents.

Births and deaths are treated together since the law governing them is very similar; marriages are discussed in a separate section.

## Births and Deaths

The legislation and regulations affecting births and deaths at sea have been examined, in an approximately chronological order, under several headings, namely: Civil Registration, British Merchant Ships, Passenger Ships and Royal Navy ships.

Under the final heading of Special Categories, miscellaneous matters, such as Colonial ships, the Partition of Ireland, Channel Islands and Isle of Man, Territorial waters, Merchant seamen, Royal Navy, Army and Wrecks are covered.

## Civil Registration

Until the introduction of civil registration in Britain there were no laws or official procedures covering the recording of births or deaths at sea.

## England and Wales

The Births and Deaths Act, 1836, which set up the system of civil registration in England and Wales, made provision for the registration of births and deaths at sea. From 1 July 1837, the captain or commanding officer of a British vessel on which the birth of a child to an English parent took place was required to make a minute[*] recording the details.[4] A certified copy of this minute was to be sent to the General Register Office (GRO)[†] where it was to be filed and a copy entered in the Marine Register Book. A similar provision[5] was made for the recording and registration of the death of any English subject aboard a British ship.

In the context of that Act, English subject should be interpreted to include Welsh. British ships would have included those of the Royal Navy and merchant ships registered not only in Britain itself but in all the dominions, colonies and overseas territories within British jurisdiction.

## Scotland

With the introduction of civil registration in Scotland, the Registration of Births, Deaths and Marriages Act (Scotland) 1854 also made provision for recording births and deaths at sea. The Act did call for the same level of detail as was required for such events on land. In practice this probably did not occur, although additional details obtained from the local registrar, or from a relative, might be added to the information supplied by the master (*see* Figure 28).

---

[*] At this date no requirement had yet been introduced for masters of merchant vessels to keep, or file, official log books.

[†] The term GRO is used throughout this book to describe the Registrar-General of Births, Deaths and Marriages to avoid confusion with the Registrar-General of Shipping and Seamen (RGSS).

From 1 January 1855, the captain or commanding officer of a British vessel on which the birth of a child to an Scottish parent took place was required to make a minute in the log book or otherwise recording the details.[6] A certified copy of this minute was to be sent to the General Registry Office (GRO) in Edinburgh where it was to be filed and a copy entered in the Marine Register Book. Unlike the English legislation there was a further provision to the effect that the GRO shall send a copy of the details to the Registrar of the parish in which the child's parents are or were last domiciled, if known, who shall enter it in his register.

A similar provision[7] was made for the recording and registration of the death of any Scottish subject aboard a British ship by its captain, transmission of details to the GRO in Edinburgh and for the GRO to send a copy of the details to the Registrar of the parish in which the deceased was domiciled, if known, who shall enter it in his register.

British ships would have included those of the Royal Navy and merchant ships registered not only in Britain itself but in all the dominions, colonies and overseas territories within British jurisdiction. In the case of Scotland it is not clear whether returns were made in respect of RN ships.

Ireland
The Registration of Births and Deaths Act (Ireland) 1863, under which the system of civil registration of births and deaths was introduced to Ireland, made provision for the recording births and deaths at sea.

From 1 January 1864, the captain or commanding officer of a British vessel on which the birth of a child to an Irish parent took place was required to make a minute in the log book or otherwise recording the details.[8] A certified copy of this minute was to be sent to the General Register Office (GRO) in Dublin where it was to be filed and a copy entered in the Marine Register Book of Births. A similar provision[9] was made for the recording and registration of the death of any Irish subject aboard a British ship and for the keeping, by the GRO in Dublin, of a Marine Register Book of Deaths.

British ships should have included those of the Royal Navy as well as merchant ships registered not only in Britain itself but also in all the dominions, colonies and overseas territories within British jurisdiction.

Naturally modifications were necessary to this legislation with the partition of Ireland – this is discussed later.

1874 onwards
The Registration of Births and Deaths Act 1874 consolidated earlier legislation related to births and deaths at sea.[10] Significant amongst its provisions were:

- Details of the birth of a child or death of a person aboard a British ship shall be entered in the log book.
- Legislation applies also where the ship is not British but carries passengers and its port of departure or destination is in the United Kingdom.
- Where the ship is a merchant vessel then details shall be reported to the Registrar-General of Shipping and Seamen (RGSS).
  - The RGSS shall send a copy of the details to the GRO in Scotland/Ireland where:
    - the father (or if the child is a bastard then the mother) of any child born is a Scottish/Irish subject
    - the deceased person is a Scottish/Irish subject
  - In all other instances the RGSS shall send details to the GRO in England.
- The captain of one of Her Majesty's ships shall, as directed by the Admiralty, send details to the appropriate GRO as would apply if the ship were a merchant ship.

No specific mention is made in this Act of the requirement for GRO (Scotland) to forward details to the appropriate local Registrar, but the procedure does seem to have continued.

The Merchant Shipping Act 1894[11] reiterates the provisions of the Registration of Births and Deaths Act 1874 related to the registration of births and deaths at sea on merchant ships. The 1894 Act, as we will see below, exempted ships trading exclusively between ports on the coasts of Scotland from the requirement to keep official log books. But the registers after this date do still contain numerous entries related to Scottish persons so presumably this happened as a result of filing a B&D1 form (*see* page 9) or the event being registered with a local registrar who certainly does currently report such events to the RSS via GRO (Scotland).

At more modern dates, a number of regulations and Statutory Instruments have been used to modify and clarify the system. Currently the registration of births and deaths at sea is controlled by the Merchant Shipping (Returns of Births and Deaths) Regulations 1979 which came into effect on 1 January 1980. This effectively calls for registration of:

- all births on UK-registered ships;
- deaths of crew of UK-registered ships whether occurring on-board or in a place abroad;
- births and deaths of citizens of the United Kingdom and Colonies on board non-UK registered ships where the ship subsequently calls at, or its voyage terminates at, a port in the UK.

Where these events relate to those normally resident in Scotland, Northern Ireland or the Republic of Ireland, a return should be made by the RSS to the relevant GRO for those countries. In all other cases the return should be made to the GRO for England and Wales.

*British Merchant ships*

Log Books

The requirement for the master to keep an official log book goes back relatively early but only for specific categories of vessel. Usually this relates to some form of tax or subsidy for their trade. Arctic and Southern whalers had, from 1786,[12] to compile a log book and surrender it to the Collector of Customs at the end of the voyage. From 1789[13] slave-ships had to keep a general log book, a copy of which was to be handed over to the port authorities on return to the UK; even earlier than this the surgeon had to keep a medical journal. From 1803[14] any ship carrying passengers had to keep a medical journal; if the ship had more than 50 people aboard, it had to carry a surgeon, and both he and the master kept official medical journals recording details of the health of both passengers and crew.

The Mercantile Marine Act 1850[15] required the master of every British ship to keep an official log book and, amongst other requirements, enter in it details of any illness of, injury to, or death of a member of the crew. This Act came into force on 1 October 1851; prior to this, many masters would, of course, have kept an unofficial log for their own reasons.

Official logs, for foreign-going[*] ships, had to be delivered up within 48 hours after arrival at the ship's final destination in the United Kingdom or discharge of the crew whichever was sooner. Official logs, for Home Trade ships, were to be delivered up within 21 days after 30th June or 31st December in each year.

The Merchant Shipping Act 1854[16] calls for lists to be made containing, amongst other information:

- the names of any member of the crew who have died, been maimed or hurt, with the times, places, causes and circumstances;
- the wages due to, and clothing and effects belonging to, any member of the crew who have died;
- the name, age and sex of every person, not being one of the crew, who dies on board, with date and cause;
- every birth which happens on board, with date, sex of the infant and names of the parents;
- every marriage with the date and names and ages of the parties.

The Merchant Shipping Act 1894[17] repeats the provisions for the keeping and filing of official log books but specifically excluded from this requirement ships employed exclusively in trading between ports on the coasts of Scotland. What, if any, impact this had on the registration of births and deaths at sea is unclear.

Instructions to masters as to how to record marriages, births and deaths at sea are included as part of every log book.[18] These repeat the appropriate sections of the Merchant Shipping Act 1894 and require the following of the master:

------

[*]  The term 'Foreign Going Ship' means 'every ship employed in trading or going between some place or places in the United Kingdom and some place or places situate beyond the following limits, that is to say, the Coasts of the United Kingdom, the Islands of Guernsey, Jersey, Sark, Alderney and Man and the Continent of Europe between the River Elbe and Brest inclusive'.

> In addition to the brief statement of the 'Cause of Death' below
> the Master should be careful to add in the body of the official-log
> *full particulars of all the circumstances attending the death*, more
> particularly in the case of murder, disappearance or suicide.
>
> If a death occurs in a port the name of the port should be given,
> and it should be stated whether the death occurred on board or in
> hospital.
>
> If a seaman dies on shore from an accident which happened, or
> from a disease which developed, while a member of the crew, it is
> desirable that an entry of death should be made.

Initially, the forms printed as part of the log book for recording deaths at sea contained a column for recording 'parents' names, if known', presumably to comply with the Scottish civil registration requirements. This information was never transferred into the registers kept by the RGSS and so could not have been sent on to any of the GROs.

Other returns

The official log book was not the only way, after 1851, in which details of births and deaths at sea could be reported. The instructions forming part of a log-book required that '...upon the arrival of the ship in port (except where the log-book itself is surrendered at the end of the voyage or the termination of the Agreement), a true copy of the entries shall be delivered on a Form B&D1...' So there will be many circumstances where a Return of Births and Deaths (the B&D1 form) will have been filed in addition to the log book.

The 'Instructions to Masters' included as part of that form[19] required a record of every birth of a child or death of a person on board ship to be made by the master of every British ship (excepting dominion or colonial ships within the jurisdiction of the Government of the British possession to which they belong) and of every foreign ship carrying passengers to or from the United Kingdom. Separate sections are to be found on the form for Births and Deaths; the latter being further subdivided into Crew, Lascars* and Persons who were not members of the Crew. A copy of the

---

* Lascars are Asiatics and East Africans employed under Agreements for Asia or East Africa, which open and terminate in Asia.

entry relating to any death appearing in the official log book had also to be included in addition to the tabular form.

The 'Instructions to Superintendents and Consular, Dominion and Colonial Officers', to whom the completed form was to be surrendered for onward transmission to the RGSS include the instruction that a return was also required in the case of a seaman who died out of the United Kingdom after he had ceased to be a member of the crew. The latter officials were also required to make a report concerning deaths on forms B&D3 or B&D5 (later those starting with the letters Inq. were used for this purpose).

Births and deaths were also recorded on crew lists. From as early as the mid-1860s provision was made on the back of the printed forms to record details of births and deaths of non-crew members (on Lists C and D) and, in addition (on Form AC), for the wages and effects of deceased crew members.

Wages and Effects

An Act for the prevention of Desertion of Seaman from British Merchant Ships trading to His Majesty's Colonies and Plantations in the West Indies 1797,[20] included within it provision for the disposal of the wages of seamen, and others, engaged on British vessels sailing from ports in Great Britain to those places. Monies due had to be lodged with the Receiver of the Sixpenny Duty for Greenwich Hospital within three months and claimed by the executors of the deceased within three years. If the money remained unclaimed after three years it was passed to the Seamen's Hospital at the port to which the ship belonged or, if none existed, then for the use of the old and disabled seamen of that port.

The Merchant Seamen's Fund Winding-up Act 1851[21] placed a responsibility on the master of a British ship, whose voyage is to terminate finally in the United Kingdom, to account for the wages and effects of any seaman who died. The master was to take charge of the wages, clothes and effects, selling them where practical by auction at the mast, and to record details in the official log.

The Merchant Shipping Act 1854[22] reiterates this responsibility but now describes a seamen as 'belonging to or sent home in a British ship'.

These, and later Acts, do require the monies to be surrendered and accounted for at the next port. For instance the Instructions to Masters printed in the log book include:

> When reporting the particulars on a Form B. & D.1, the master is also, if so required to give account of any moneys due to a deceased seaman or apprentice, of any deductions from his wages, and of his clothes and effects, on the relevant Form W. & E.1, C.15 or C.C.15

*Passenger ships*

The provisions described above for Civil Registration, and for British Merchant Ships apply equally to all British ships whether carrying passengers or not. There are however two specific sets of legislative provisions that apply specifically to passenger ships.

Non-British Passenger ships

All the legislation (described above under the heading of Civil Registration) concerning the recording and registration of births and deaths on board British ships was applicable, from 1874, to non-British ships whose port of departure or port of destination was within the United Kingdom.

The Merchant Shipping Act 1970 modified these requirements further[23]. Now all foreign-registered ships, calling at a UK port during or at the end of their voyage, are required to make a return of any births or deaths of citizens of the UK or Colonies.

As the requirement, under UK law, to keep and file an official log book would not seem to apply to such ships, the method by which these events were reported would presumably have been the B&D1 form already described since this requirement did apply to such vessels.

Passenger Lists

The Passenger Act 1855[24] required the master of every ship bringing passengers into the United Kingdom from any place out of Europe and not within the Mediterranean Sea to make a list of passengers. This was to include a list showing those who died, with supposed cause, or who were born on the voyage. This list was to be filed with an emigration or customs official who was to pass the details on to the GRO, who was to file the information and record it in the Marine Register Book.

Masters were reminded, on the forms provided, that they were also required to make an entry in the official log and make the appropriate return to the RGSS. Passenger Lists dated after Acts[25] of 1905 and 1906 remind the master that passengers joining the vessel within Europe must be included on the list.

As a result of a request from the Irish Administration in Dublin, who were clearly worried at the prospect of Irish revolutionary agitators infiltrating into the country from America, an instruction was given in December 1858 to the authorities at UK ports to transmit to the Lord Lieutenant in Ireland copies of the lists of passengers arriving from North America. The forwarding was discontinued in June 1870.

Another section of the Passenger Act 1855[26] called upon the master of every ship* carrying passengers out from the United Kingdom to deliver two lists of passengers to the Officer of Customs who was to retain one and return the other to the master. The master was required to enter upon the latter list (known as the Master's List) details of any births or deaths that occurred on the voyage. He was to deposit it on arrival, and landing of the passengers, in a foreign port either with HM's Consul or with the Chief Officer of Customs if the port was in a British possession.

*Royal Navy ships*
The recording of births and deaths aboard His/Her Majesty's ships was covered by King's/Queen's Regulations and Admiralty Instructions, which were regularly updated. By 1909[27] the Admiralty was requiring the captain to record details in the log book and to send a certified copy of the details on Form S-554 to the appropriate GRO, this being defined as:

- births of the children of an English or Welsh father, and the deaths of English or Welsh subjects, to the GRO in London;

---

\* Ships belonging to the Royal Navy or the East India Company were exempt from this legislation.

- births of the children of a Scottish father, and the deaths of Scottish subjects, to the GRO in Edinburgh;

- births of the children of an Irish father, and the deaths of Irish subjects, to the GRO in Dublin.

- If the nationality of the father of a child born on board, or the nationality of a person who has died on board, cannot be satisfactorily ascertained, the return was to be sent to the GRO in London.

The return was also to be sent in the event of the death of an officer or man whilst absent on special active service.

It should be noted that these instructions differ from the legislative requirements in two respects. Firstly the legislation required that returns related to all persons (and parents of children) who were not Scottish or Irish subjects should be sent to the GRO in London even if their nationality could be determined. For instance if such a person is known to be (say) French then the legislation requires the GRO in London to be informed but these Admiralty Instructions seem to call for no return. Secondly no mention is made in the Admiralty Instructions of the legal requirement to consider the nationality of the mother in the case of a bastard child. These returns were made on Form S-554.

Earlier Admiralty Instructions[28] set out what information was to be recorded about deaths at sea, calling up the forms printed as appendixes to the appropriate civil registration acts – this of course meant that more information was required about Scotsmen than Englishmen. Form S-554, which was in use by 1909, makes no provision for the inclusion of that additional information.

Log books were to be filed with the Admiralty.

*Special categories*
Colonial ships
In the Instructions to Masters, printed as part of merchant ship log books, it is stated that the regulations related to births and deaths at sea do not apply to dominion or colonial ships within the jurisdiction of the Government of the British possession to which they belong. In the Instructions regarding the return of Births and Deaths (Form B&D1) it is stated that the masters of colonial vessels exclusively employed

in the colonial coasting trade are excluded from the regulations. A point which is very similar to, but not absolutely identical to, that made in the notes associated with the log book.

Some colonies, Australia in particular, had their own legislation, and some practical information on this is given in the chapter on Registrars-General of Births, Deaths and Marriages.

## Partition of Ireland

Following the creation of the Irish Free State in 1922, the appropriate sections of the Merchant Shipping Act 1894 continued in force in relation to Irish-registered ships and the Irish authorities reported births and deaths of British subjects to the RGSS on Form B&D1 (Irish).[29] This did not seem to continue for long and no such reports are received now. The GRO (England and Wales) holds only a *Report by the Irish Free State to the General Register Office of events at sea* recording births and deaths at sea dated 1924.[30] The RGSS though does still report births and deaths aboard British ships of Irish citizens to the GRO in Dublin as described above.

Admiralty Regulations[31] were also changed so that records of all events involving a person from Ireland should include a note of their place of birth so that where the deceased person, or the parent of a child, was:

- born in Northern Ireland, the return should be sent to GRO in Belfast.

- born in the Irish Free State, the return should be sent to GRO in Dublin.

Where the place of birth was not known then a return should be sent to both GROs.

## Channel Isles and Isle of Man

Onward-reporting arrangements, from the RGSS to the GRO for the Isle of Man only came into force in 1980. No such arrangements exist for any of the Channel Islands.

## Territorial waters

Where a death took place in territorial waters it should have been registered by the local Registrar of Deaths. The local registrar, when querying as to whether he was correct in registering the death of James Percival who had died aboard the *SS Morea* off Southend on 17th March 1922, was informed[32] that '... as the death occurred in territorial waters it was rightly registered by you'. But total reliance should not be placed on this since, for example, following the loss of the *SS J. M. Lennard* in Goole Reach in August 1894, the deaths resulting from the tragedy were registered in the Marine Deaths Register and not locally. Perhaps the difference in this case may have been that bodies were not recovered and so never brought ashore; alternatively it may be because the deaths occurred beyond the low-water mark which is sometimes considered to be the limits of a registration district.

There would seem to be a clear clash of regulations here since events occurring within a local registrar's jurisdiction should indeed be registered by him – and territorial waters would seem to be within such a jurisdiction. But an event on board a ship must be registered by the RGSS.

Presumably in the case of a birth aboard a ship in territorial waters, a similar clash of regulations would apply.

## Merchant seamen

In addition to the legislation summarised above there are several Acts[33] related to the relief and support of disabled seamen and their dependants. From 1747, these required the masters or owners of merchant ships to keep a Muster Roll entering in it details of all officers, seamen and other persons employed on the vessel. The keeper of the Muster Roll was required to deliver up a copy to the Seamen's Fund Receiver at the port of departure. The master was then to continue the roll, by marking up his own copy, with any discharges, desertions, any new crew and any injuries or deaths. A duplicate of this continuation roll was to be delivered to the Receiver at the end of the voyage, who was then to send it to the Governors of the Seamen's Fund in London, having first made a further copy for retention locally.[34] An Act of 1834[35] required a record to be kept of the effects left by, and wages due to, dead or deserted seamen. These Acts were finally repealed in 1851.[36]

## Royal Navy

Royal Navy officers are reminded by Admiralty Instructions[37] that:

- If an officer or man dies aboard an RN vessel then RN procedures are followed.

- If an officer or man dies aboard a hospital ship then the master will follow the procedures for a merchant vessel.

If the body of an officer or man is taken ashore then it is not required to inform the local (shore) authorities as the person had not died in their jurisdiction.

## Army

A note on a Ministry of Transport, Marine Division, file[38] makes the following points:

> (1) If a Passenger dies on a Passenger Ship the Captain makes an entry in the Official Log describing if possible the cause of death. He reports to the proper Authorities or Officials at the next port of call, and hands over the effects of the Passenger, which are sent to the Treasury to be passed to the next of Kin. The usual Forms in the Captain's possession are filled in.
>
> (2) In the case of a Soldier dying on a Passenger Ship, the fact is recorded in the Log, and the same formalities are gone through as in the case of a Passenger (vide. Paragraph No. 1) with the addition that the Captain must make a statement and hand it to the Military, Naval or other Authorities at the next port of call if abroad, if in England, at the Custom House.
>
> (3) If a Soldier dies on a Troop Ship, the fact is recorded in the Official Log, the Medical Officer gives a certificate as to the cause of death, and the Captain at his next port of call must appear before the Military or Naval Authorities and make a sworn declaration with regard to the occurrence. *[N.B. the Military or Naval authorities will then advise the War Office.]*
>
> (4) As regards a Seaman dying on board ship, the same formalities must be gone through as in the case of the death of a Passenger.

<u>Wrecks</u>

The Merchant Shipping Act 1854[39] appointed a Receiver of Wreck and placed upon him, or in his absence any Justice of the Peace, the duty to examine 'any person belonging to any ship which may have been in distress on the Coasts of the United Kingdom'. Two copies of the written examination were to be made; one was to be sent to the Board of Trade, the other to the secretary of Lloyds in London.

The standard form on which a deposition was recorded provides for details of the incident and, under item 16, details of any loss of life but, only in rare instances, are names recorded.

The loss of a Royal Navy ship would result in an enquiry that by custom consisted of the court martial of the captain or surviving officers.

**Marriages**

*Merchant Ships*

There is no provision in law for the master of a British merchant vessel to perform a marriage ceremony.[40] But the Merchant Shipping Act 1854[41] did place a clear requirement on the master to record any marriage taking place on board his ship in the official log; this was re-enacted in the Merchant Shipping Act 1894.[42] Neither Act applies to foreign-registered vessels.

The instruction printed as part of the log book remind the master of this situation in clear terms:

> **MARRIAGES.** — Section 240(6) of the Merchant Shipping Act, 1894, requires the master of the Ship to enter in his Official Log the particulars of every Marriage that has taken place on board. Masters are reminded that they have no power to perform the marriage ceremony on board their vessels, and that if such ceremony is performed by them the marriage will not be a legal one.

Despite this, there has long been a popular belief that such marriages were legal and the files of the Board of Trade and Registrar-General[43] reflect the on-going debate over this issue. It would appear though, that in response to an enquiry from the GRO for England and Wales in 1934,[44] the RGSS could find no cases in recent years of any marriage on a British merchant ship solemnised by the master. Clearly he had not looked as far back as 1905 as the GRO's files[45] contain a debate about the legality of the marriage solemnised by the master, aboard the *County of Dumfries* off Pitcairn Island at 1:30 p.m. on 23rd April 1905, between two Islanders, Walter Henry Petch and Esther Godfrey.

As a final comment resulting from that correspondence[44] the Treasury Solicitor observes 'that there is another, and a more difficult, question which may eventually have to be decided, vizt. the position where a marriage is solemnized in the presence of an episcopally ordained priest on a merchant vessel otherwise than by special licence'; no conclusion on that point was reached.

The above does assume that English law applies. However Scottish law recognises certain forms of irregular marriage,[46] including those by cohabitation with repute and, until 1940, by consent in the presence of witnesses (by declaration). A shipboard ceremony might therefore perhaps be used as evidence in support of the validity of such an irregular marriage under Scottish law.

An interesting discussion, from the layman's viewpoint, of the law related to marriages at sea is to be found in an short article of that title by Arthur S May[47] published in 1932 in *The Seaman*, the official organ of the International Seafarers and of the National Sailors' & Firemen's Union (official organ of the National Union of Seamen).

As well as in log books, marriages might also be recorded on crew lists. From as early as the 1863 provision was made on the back of the printed forms to record details of any marriages.

## Special Licences
There has been provision, under Canon Law, for licences to be issued for the solemnising of marriages since at least the sixteenth century. The relevance here is that they authorise the performance of the ceremony in a place other than that in which one of the parties resides. Special licences, necessary where the ceremony was to be performed at a place outside the dioceses where either party resided, could be issued by the officials of the two Archbishops, namely of Canterbury and York. The Archbishop of York could issue such a licence for a ceremony anywhere in the Northern Province; the Archbishop of Canterbury anywhere in England and Wales. In addition the Bishop of London has jurisdiction overseas although this did not

cover all territories at all dates; in particular it did not extend to most British colonies who had acquired their own bishops in the 19th century.[48]

There would therefore seem to a possibility that marriage licences may have been issued under such ecclesiastical authority for marriages at sea.[*]

*Royal Navy*
Admiralty Instructions[49] set out how the Royal Navy reports marriages at sea:

> ...the Captain is, when marriages are solemnized on board the Ship he commands out of the United Kingdom, to cause a declaration of the marriage, signed by the Minister of the Church... ..to be entered in the log book. And he is to transmit to the Admiralty a certified copy of such declaration, which will be forwarded to the Registrar of the Consistory Court of the Lord Bishop of London, in Doctor's Commons, for the purpose of being registered.

This instruction seems to have been amended in 1880[50] when the Admiralty directed that returns should be sent directly to the GRO for England and Wales. At that date they also caused certified copied of previous entries to be forwarded from the Bishop of London's registry to the GRO.

Clearly though there must have been some question earlier as to the legality of this procedure as the Consular Marriage Act 1849[51] confirms the legality of marriages, where one or both of the parties is a British subject, performed on board a British vessel of war on any foreign station by a Minister in Holy Orders in the presence of the officer commanding such vessel.

No mention is made though, in the quoted Admiralty Instruction, about the performance of marriage ceremonies by the captain himself. It seems as if, unlike the situation with their civilian counterparts, that it was an accepted practice for the captain of a Royal Navy ship to be permitted to solemnise a marriage; the Abstract

---

[*] The authors know of no such examples but have not made any attempt to locate any marriage licences bonds amongst these records.

of Arrangements referred to does make mention of marriages being performed by the captains of RN ships. The Confirmation of Marriages on HM Ships Act 1879[52] was enacted to legalise all such marriages, performed before that date, where both parties were British subjects. The Marriage Act 1890[53] subsequently made legal the performance of a marriage on board an HM vessel on foreign station, where one or both parties was British, by the captain as if he were a consul. Just what the legal position was between 1880 and 1890 is unclear, as they were not covered by either the 1879 or 1890 Acts. The Foreign Marriages Act 1892[54] altered the situation yet again by requiring that the commanding officer of such a vessel should hold a marriage warrant issued by a Secretary of State.

**A cautionary tale!**

In the section above on Births and Deaths: Royal Navy, it has been pointed out that the legislation may not always be followed fully in practice. Perhaps a, hopefully extreme, example of this is brought to our attention by a file note in the RGSS policy files related to deaths:[55]

> In 1957, 7,000 log books were received for ships registered at Hong Kong. Some of the cases were registered but owing to the amount of work involved and the unlikelihood of applications for certificates being received it was decided by Mr. Peaty that they should not be indexed or registered. If applications for certificates are received send for the log book and register in the usual way.
>
> vmc 21/1/1958

So in our searching we should be guided by what the legislation and regulations required of officials but we would be unwise to assume that they always followed them slavishly or precisely. The following five chapters describe what records are extant (that is were actually created and have survived) under the headings of Merchant Ships, Registrar-General of Shipping and Seamen, Royal Navy, Admiralty and Registrars-General of Births, Deaths and Marriages.

# MERCHANT SHIPS

## Introduction

In the chapter on Legislation and Regulations we discovered just what records should have been created. Now we will look at just what has survived and over what period, what it contains, where it is to be found, and how it is arranged.

This chapter is concerned with primary sources related to events that occurred aboard British merchant ships and passenger ships, of any nationality, to or from the UK. Later chapters will address primary sources for Royal Navy ships and the secondary sources compiled by the Registrar-General of Shipping and Seamen, the Admiralty and the General Register Offices.

Certain material mentioned in the chapter on Legislation and Regulations is known not to survive, and we may therefore dismiss any further consideration of it; namely:

- The certified copies of the minute, or log book entry, sent by the master of a British vessel to the appropriate General Register Office survive only for Scotland. The original minute may possibly survive, the log book should survive, the appropriate GRO's entry in the Marine Register survives but the certified copy referred to in the legislation does not survive except for those sent to GRO (Scotland).[*]

- Details of births and deaths, extracted from inward passenger lists, sent by emigration or customs officials to the appropriate General Register Office do not survive. The original passenger list may possibly survive, the log book should survive, the appropriate GRO's entry in the Marine Register survives but the copy referred to in the legislation does not.

---

[*] These are probably in the series of 'Intimations' at GRO (Scotland) - *see* pages 100 and 101.

## Muster Rolls

Survival of the Muster Rolls, required by the Act for the Relief and Support of maimed and disabled seamen, 1746, is somewhat patchy. These are mostly to be found at TNA in PRO series *Agreements and Crew Lists, Series I (BT 98)* where they survive for the period 1747-1834 for only a few ports, namely:

| Port | Start Date |
|---|---|
| Shields and other Northern Ports | 1747 |
| Plymouth | 1761 |
| Dartmouth | 1770 |
| Liverpool | 1772 |
| Other ports | from 1800 |

A few muster rolls survive in other series, for example those for Plymouth (1776-1780) are in CUST 66/27 and those for Scarborough (1747-1765) are in CUST 91/111-112 and it is possible that others still await discovery. Additionally a few early muster books can be found in local record offices; for example Whitby Museum holds muster books for Whitby ships, 1708-1805 and 1835-1838. From 1835 onwards, until their abolition in 1851, their usefulness is eclipsed by the crew lists introduced in that year – these are described below.

Provision is made for the recording, against each man's name, of:

• Time when and Place where Discharged, Run, Dead, Killed, Slain or Drowned

• Time when and Place where Hurt or Wounded

Naturally only those filed at the end of a voyage would be expected to contain any reference to deaths of seamen.

Unfortunately there are no simple indexes to the names in these muster books and they are arranged by year and port of filing. Sometimes they include a full list of the crew's names, but more commonly name only the master and identify the number of crew members.

## Log Books

The key, primary, source that you should endeavour to locate is the ship's official log book. An entry in it will have been made at the time of the event and should give more details than any of the other sources and, hopefully, be the most accurate. Due to both their location and their lack of indexes it may though be more convenient to use some of the secondary sources initially such as the registers compiled by the RGSS and GROs.

Whilst it must surely have been the normal practice for the masters of merchant vessels to keep log books, there is no comprehensive collection of them until the legal requirement, introduced in 1851, for their compilation and retention. Some early examples of them will no doubt be found both at local record offices, in the collections of various maritime museum archives and, at TNA, in the records of the High Court of Admiralty. Finding anything of direct relevance to one's researches must be considered serendipitous.

From Oct 1851 onwards the master of every British ship (and that would include those registered in the colonies) was required to create and file an official log book. These should contain details of:

| From | Categories included |
|---|---|
| 1 July 1837 | • births to English/Welsh fathers<br><br>• deaths of English/Welsh subjects<br><br>These requirements may have been interpreted not to cover crew.<br><br>Details may have been entered in any appropriate documentation until 1854. |
| 1 Oct 1851 | • Deaths of crew members, recording wages and the proceeds from the sale of their effects. |
| 1854 | • All marriages<br><br>• All births and deaths |

But after 1894:

- Ships employed exclusively in trading between ports on the coasts of Scotland were exempt from the requirements to keep log books.

- Regulations related to births and deaths at sea do not apply to dominion or colonial ships within the jurisdiction of the Government of the British possession to which they belong.

- Particulars of deaths of seamen who have been discharged sick, or who from other cause have recently left British vessels, should be included.

The log book had to be delivered to the Registrar-General of Shipping and Seaman within 48 hours after arrival at the ship's final destination in the UK (Foreign-going ships) or within 21 days after 30th June or 31st December in each year (Home Trade ships).

Official log books (which were a legal requirement from 1 October 1851) begin to appear amongst the records from that date, though many have been destroyed; usually only those recording a birth, marriage or death have survived.

There is a separate series at TNA, *Ships' Official Logs (BT 165)*, that nominally covers the period 1857-1972 although the majority of logs therein are from the period 1902 to 1919. Log books for 1902-1912 were preserved in that series where they contained entries of birth, marriage or death; also to be found there are all the surviving logs for the period 1914-1919. Selected logs for 1913 are in series BT 99. Others logs are mostly to be found with the Agreements and Crew Lists at TNA or elsewhere; a list of where to look for these is in Appendix 1.

BT 165 is arranged mostly by year and then ship's Official Number.[*] BT 165/2035 is particular strong in logs containing marriages and the box contains a list where somebody, probably in 1978, has attempted to bring this information together for the period 1857-1864. With the exception of this there are no indexes to events contained in the log books in this series and the secondary sources compiled by the RGSS and GROs need to be used.

---

[*] From 1857 onwards, each ship was allocated an Official Number on registration; these numbers were retained for the life of the ship, were not reused and may be found from the *Mercantile Navy List*.

## WAGES AND EFFECTS DETAILS

- Reference number in Agreement
- Christian and Surname of Deceased
- Certificates, if any:
    - Description. State whether Mate's, Engineer's, Naval Reserve &c
    - Numbers
    - Net amount of Wages and total Proceeds of Sale of Effects paid to Superintendent, Officer of Customs or Consul as per Account in Form W.&E.1
    - Particulars of Effects (if any) delivered to Superintendent, Officer of Customs or Consul as per Account in Form W.&E.1

## BIRTH DETAILS

- Date of birth
- Name of child (if any)
- Sex
- Name and surname of father (or mother if child illegitimate)
- Rank, profession or occupation of father (or mother if child illegitimate)
- Name and surname of mother
- Father: Nationality (stating birthplace)
- Father: Last place of abode
- Mother: Nationality (stating birthplace)
- Mother: Last place of abode
- Signature of father or mother
- Signature of master, mate or crew member
- Port and country at which report is made
- Signature and Title of Officer to whom reported

## MARRIAGE DETAILS

- Date when married
- Christian and surnames of both parties
- State whether Single, Widow or Widower
- Profession or Occupation
- Father's Christian and Surname
- Profession or Occupation of Father

## DEATH DETAILS

There are separate sections on the forms for:

- Crew, including master, on European Agreement
- Crew and others on Asiatic Agreement
- Non-members of Crew

- Date of death
- Place of death
- Name and surname of deceased
- Sex
- Age
- Rating or Rank, Profession or Occupation
- Nationality (stating birthplace)
- Last place of abode
- Cause of death
- Signature of master or person in charge
- Signature of mate or member of crew
- Signature of surgeon or medical practitioner if any.
- Port and country at which report is made
- Signature and Title of Officer to whom reported

Table 1: Contents of forms

The precise arrangement of the information within the log book depends on its date and the type of voyage, but most will contain two components. The first is a pre-printed table in which the information required by law must be recorded; this is normally subdivided into sections for Marriages, Births and Deaths, the latter being categorised according to Members of crew (other than Lascars) but including masters; Lascars; Non-members of crew. There may also be a section on the Wages and Effects of deceased seamen and apprentices. The information that each section should contain is given in Table 1.

The second component, in the body of the log, will give details of the event and, in the case of a death, the circumstances surrounding it; a burial at sea will usually be recorded here. Full details of the effects of a deceased seaman may also be listed. Sample entries are to be found in Figures 1 to 3.

The captains of East India Company ships were required to record births, deaths and marriages that took place on board their vessels. Log books and journals of East Indiamen,[56] of which there are some 3,822, should be sought amongst the Oriental and India Office Collections at the British Library. Series L/MAR/B covers the period 1702-1834 and these contain lists of both outward and inward passengers. Other marine records, such as L/MAR/C/ 887, do include lists of passengers to and from India in various ships, 1838-1858.

Log books of Hudson's Bay Company ships often contain lists of passengers and crew. Mostly these are to be found in *Section C. Ships' Records* but a few, including some East Indiamen, are in *Section E. Private Records*. There is a good on-line finding aid at www.gov.mb.ca/chc/archives/hbca/resource/ The original records are at the Archives of Manitoba but microfilm copies are to be found at the National Archives of Canada and TNA (Section C only in series BH1).

## Crew Lists

Crew lists should not be overlooked as a primary source for information on births and deaths at sea for several reasons. Naturally one would expect to find recorded there, since their inception in 1835, information about the death of seamen given under the headings 'Time of death or leaving ship', 'Place where' and 'How disposed of'; Figure 4 shows such an example.

Births and deaths of non-crew members, who were English subjects, had to be recorded in the ship's documentation from 1 July 1837. Since this was prior to the introduction of ship's official logs it may be that the crew list was the place chosen by the master for this purpose. Examples of consular annotations, on the back of crew lists, concerning deaths can be found from at least as early as 1845. Provision was made on the printed forms (List C) from 1854 to record the wages and effects of deceased seamen.

From 1863 provision was being made on the back of the printed forms (Lists C and D) to record details of births and deaths of non-crew members. So, whatever the date, it would be prudent to check the crew lists for any such events taking place at sea, whether involving a crew member or a passenger. The information to be found on these forms is listed in Table 1. An example is shown in Figure 5.

All Agreements and Crew Lists from 1835 to 1976 have been preserved, but after that date only a 10% sample remain. The location of these records is given in Appendix 1.

From 1835 to 1844 the lists, which are at TNA in series BT 98, are arranged by Port of Registry and then alphabetically in boxes according to the ship's name. From 1845 to 1856 the arrangement is by year that the voyage ended, port of registry and then ship's name. From 1857 onwards the arrangement is again by year and then ship's official number. There are a few exceptions to this arrangement for some special categories of vessel. For fuller details on the arrangement and content of these records see one of the two standard works on the subject[57].

In general there are very few indexes to the names in crew lists and only one to the births or deaths* recorded on them. One ongoing set of transcripts and indexes, being published on CD-ROM by Family History Indexes, covers on a county-by-county† basis crew lists for 1851. Being a full transcript these allows searches to be made not only by name but also by terms such as 'dead' or 'drowned'.

Whilst details of all deaths recorded on crew lists, prior to 1874, should have been reported directly to the General Register Office it would be unwise to rely on this. A check made in the Marine Deaths Index, for England and Wales, for the 12 seamen discharged as dead from Cornish ships in 1851, all of whom gave places of birth in England, failed to reveal any of them. It may be that the legislation requiring reporting of deaths was thought not to apply to crew.

**Consular records**

Those who have closely examined articles, agreements, crew lists and log books will have noticed the consular stamps thereon. Deposit of documents with consuls was the normal practice from at least 1845. Whilst mostly no detailed record survives of this that will assist, there is some material related to ships arriving and departing from Archangel amongst its consular archives (PRO FO 267). These consist of lists of ships, articles and agreement covering the period 1836-1889; in the remarks columns notes can be found recording deaths on the voyage. The example below is taken from a Register of Ship's Articles, received by the consul at Archangel, 1857-1866 (FO 267/28); this entry is dated 1858:

---

\* A list of deaths recorded on those crew lists held at the Cheshire Record Office, is to be found there catalogued under "NS". Their holdings comprise approximately 80% of those for ships registered at Runcorn for the period 1863-1913

† At the time of writing those for ships with ports of registry in Aberdeenshire, Angus, Cornwall, Renfrewshire, Scotland South-East and Scotland South-West, Highlands & Islands have been published.

| No | Ships Name | Port of register | Official No | Name of Master | from whence | |
|---|---|---|---|---|---|---|
| 131 | Warbler | Belfast | 19432 | Thº Patton | Liverpool | |

| Whither bound | Date Arrival | | of Departure | | Remarks |
|---|---|---|---|---|---|
| Leghorn | Aug | 2 | Sept | 4 | Robert Anderson died on voyage out ...... |

## Return of Births and Deaths (B&D1) forms

The official log book was not the only way, after 1851, in which details of births and deaths at sea could be reported. Upon arrival of the ship in port, unless the log book itself was to be surrendered, at the end of the voyage or the termination of the Agreement, a true copy of the entries had to be delivered on a Form B&D1. This applied to all British ships (excepting dominion or colonial ships within the jurisdiction of the Government of the British possession to which they belonged) and to any foreign ship carrying passengers to or from the United Kingdom. A form was required in the case of a seaman dying outside the United Kingdom after ceasing to be a member of the crew.

These forms survive for the periods 1914-1919 and 1939-1964 and are preserved at the National Maritime Museum where they are arranged in three series; they are sometimes described as 'Returns of Death', although they do record births as well:

- January 1914 to 1919
  These are arranged by date (year and month) then alphabetically by vessel's name. There is also a single box of Births to Passengers, January - June 1915.

- 1939-1945
  These are arranged by date (year and month) then alphabetically by vessel's name; there are separate series for crew and passengers

- 1946-1964

  These are arranged date (year and month) then alphabetically by vessel's name; there are separate series for crew and passengers.

No returns exist between 1920 and 1938; those from 1965 to the present day are held at the RSS. There are some gaps in these records.

On a B&D1 form is recorded the name, official number and port of registry of the ship together with, for a death, the date and place of death, name, age, rank/occupation, address and cause of death of deceased. On the reverse of the form there should be an extract of the ship's log book giving an account of the events that led to any death at sea; log book extracts are not always included. Sometimes, especially in the 1914-1919 series, supporting papers giving the circumstances surrounding a death (such as papers from the Embassy or Consulate) may be attached. The information to be found on these forms is listed in Table 1. For an example *see* Figure 6.

The series for 1939-1945 contains details of many deaths aboard hospital ships, often at ports in the Indian subcontinent. Many researchers may overlook these not believing that such deaths would be classified as 'at sea'.

B&D1 forms also make provision for reporting births at sea, but such events are much rarer than deaths at sea and almost exclusively limited to passenger vessels.

**Casualty and Death (C&D) Lists**

Where the vessel has been lost at sea then any crew agreements and log book would not have survived. In such circumstances the owners of the vessel were required to send the copy of the crew list retained ashore prior to its departure (the 'Red Copy') to the RGSS. *Casualty and Deaths Lists (C&D)* would be used for the registration of the deaths of the crew members; some of these documents may be found in the various series of crew lists. The National Maritime Museum holds these for 1920-1933 in a single series, covering the whole period, arranged by ships' official numbers; these include casualties and deaths on fishing vessel's (List D) for the same period. Many C&D lists are included with the 1939-1950 log books and crew agreements at TNA.

**Wages and Effects of Deceased Seamen**

Although, as a consequence of an Act of 1834, masters were required to keep a record of the effects left by, and wages due to, deceased seamen nothing seems to have survived that early.

From 1 October 1851 though, as a consequence of the Mercantile Marine Act 1850, the master of a British ship had to take charge of the wages and effects of any seaman who died, selling these where practical by auction at the mast, and recording details in the official log. When reporting the particulars of the death on a Form B&D1, the master was also required to give account of any moneys due to the deceased seaman or apprentice, of any deductions from his wages, and of his clothes and effects, on the relevant form W&E1, C15 or CC15.

No specific collections of these forms have been found though it is possible that some may be found amongst the collections of B&D1 forms described above. Other details may be found by searching the log books and crew lists (*see* above) or the *Registers of Wages and Effects of Deceased Seamen (BT 153)* – *see* the next chapter on the records of the Registrar-General of Shipping and Seamen.

**Inquiry Reports**

When the master of a vessel filed a B&D1 form with a Superintendent of Mercantile Marine, Consular, Dominion or Colonial Officer, for forwarding to the RGSS, then those officials were required to make and file a report. These reports were on forms B&D3, B&D5 or those beginning Inq. – the number depending on which type of official, which trade the vessel was in and even whether the master gave details under oath or after making a declaration.

Such reports as do survive are to be found in *Inquiries into Deaths at Sea, Papers and Reports (BT 341)*. These documents contain statements, log book entries, medical reports and other relevant information regarding the particular death at sea. Inquiries may relate to crew or passengers; the period covered is 1939-1946 plus the year 1964. The series is arranged by year and then alphabetically by ship's names. The Returns of Death that originally accompanied these papers are now held at the NMM - *see* Return of Births and Deaths (B&D1) forms above.

## Passenger Lists

*Arrivals*
From 1855 the master of every ship bringing passengers into the United Kingdom from any place out of Europe and not within the Mediterranean Sea had to file a list of passengers; this was to include a list showing those who died, with supposed cause, or who were born on the voyage. Passenger lists dated after subsequent Acts in 1905 and 1906 remind the master that passengers joining the vessel within Europe must be included on the list. Masters were reminded, on the forms provided, that they were also required to make an entry in the official log and make the appropriate return to the RGSS.

The series *Passenger Lists, Inward (BT 26)* contains the surviving lists for the periods 1878-1888 and 1890-1960; those prior to 1878 were destroyed in error long ago and those after 1960 have not been preserved. The series is arranged by year and port of arrival. As it is vast and there is no index to names, it is essential to have the name of a ship, its port of arrival and an approximate date. The date and ship's name may usually be found from the secondary sources described in the following chapters. The *Register of Passenger Lists (BT 32)*, *Lloyds Register* or *Lloyd's List* may assist in determining the port of arrival.

For the period December 1858 to June 1870 the port authorities sent copies of these passenger lists to Ireland. These now survive in the National Archives in Dublin. With a few exceptions, the lists are to be found in two records series, namely: *Chief Secretary for Ireland's Office, Unregistered Papers* (December 1858 to 1867) and *Chief Secretary for Ireland's Office, Registered Papers* (1868 to June 1870). The material surviving there is not comprehensive.

Gaps in the survival of these records can be filled by consulting either the log book for the ship or the secondary source *Registers of Births, Deaths and Marriages of Passengers at Sea (BT 158)* described in the chapter Registrar-General of Shipping and Seamen and in Appendix 2 Table 4 and 5.

The births section normally records the name of the infant, sex, name of parents and nationality. The deaths section normally records the name of the deceased, sex, age, occupation, nationality and cause of death. In neither case is the date or place of the event recorded, but this should have been entered in the log book. An example taken from a inward passenger list is shown in Figure 7.

*Departures*

The passenger lists filed on departure from the UK will not, of course, contain details of any events at sea as those are in the future. But the copy, known as the Master's List, that under UK law should have been filed at the destination port ought to contain this information.

Where the port of destination was in a British colony or possession then the list had to be filed with the Chief Officer of Customs. Any surviving records are likely to have remained locally and be found in the appropriate state or national archive. It is also possible, but unlikely, that some records await discovery amongst the various Colonial and Dominion Office series of records, but so far none has been found.

Where the port of destination was in a foreign country, then the list had to be filed with HM's Consul. One might expect to find these in the appropriate consular series of Foreign Office records at TNA, but so far none have been discovered.[58]

*Other Countries*

Many counties have their own requirements for the filing of passenger lists for arriving ships and these lists, like those for the UK, are likely to record any births and deaths that had occurred during the voyage. Thus it is wise to search for such records in the archives of the country of arrival and perhaps also that where the ship was registered.

It is really beyond the scope of this book to survey the appropriate holdings of the archives of every nation – but here we will mention a few possibilities.

**Argentina:** Passenger lists, and other arrival records, for the port of Buenos Aires, from 1821 to 15 May 1869 are to be found in the Department of Written Documents at the National Archives (Archivo General de la Nación). These are arranged in volumes by year, under the name of the ship. These volumes record: name of ship, date entered port (day, month, year), port of embarkation, and names of passengers. Where families arrived with children, it was quite common that the children were not listed; also the wife was not usually listed by name, but simply as '... y sra' (and wife).

Those for the period 1882 to April 1926, for Buenos Aires, are to be found at the Centros de Estudios Migratorios de Latinoamericos (CEMLA) where they are available on microfilm and as a database.

Those for the period 1870-1881 seem to have been lost.

It should be remembered that many persons coming to Buenos Aires may have actually disembarked at Montevideo in Uruguay.

**Australia:** Early UK and colonial legislation, as well as the UK Merchant Shipping Act 1894, required passenger lists to be filed. These requirements continued following independence and were incorporated into Part V of the Navigation Act 1912 which became effective on 1 October 1923 when the Navigation (Passengers) Regulations were passed. These called for a 'Report of Passengers from Parts beyond the Commonwealth [of Australia]'. Details of births and deaths on the voyage were normally noted on incoming passenger lists.

Passenger lists from 1924 onwards are held in the various offices of the National Archives of Australia – details of their holdings can be found in the facts sheets available on their website at www.naa.gov.au. Records prior to 1924 are held by the various state archives (*see* below) or by one of the regional offices of the National Archives of Australia; the latter's holdings are listed in their guide for family historians.[59] The records are arranged by port and then date of arrival. The starting dates vary considerably according to port – the earliest surviving ones being for Brisbane 1852.

In addition there are significant collections of inward passenger lists to be found in the various state archives. For example, preserved at State Records, New South Wales,[60] are the series of *Passengers arriving (*or *Shipping lists,* or *Passenger lists), 1855-1922, CGS 13278* – these sometimes mention events at sea but not consistently. Also to be found there are the *Colonial Secretary: Reports of Vessels Arrived (Shipping Reports), 1826 to April 1859,* these contain details of dates and causes of death during the voyage.[61] *Reports by the Immigration Agent on condition of immigrants and ships on their arrival, 1837-95, CGS 5255,* sometimes provide details of deaths at sea; the volumes are indexed by ship's name.

*Reports by surgeons on health of immigrants during their passage (Medical Journals), 1838-86, CGS 5256*, include detailed records of deaths, diseases, and illnesses on the voyage.

Preserved at State Records of South Australia is the series of *Immigrant Ships' Papers (GRG 35/48)* (1849-1867 and 1873-1885); these contain details of births and deaths on board.[62]

No doubt other series survive in the various state and territory archives.

**Canada:** Passenger lists for ships arriving at ports in Canada were systematically retained from 1865 onwards. Those for the period 1865-1935 are at the National Archives of Canada; they are available on microfilm there and in a number of other locations. Post-1935 lists are still with Citizenship and Immigration Canada who will provide details for a fee, in response to a request on the appropriate form, from a Canadian citizen or an individual present in Canada. Addresses and further details about both sets of records are to be found on the website of the National Archives of Canada at www.archives.ca. The records are mostly arranged by port and date of arrival, so it is necessary to know this information, in addition to the ship's name, before embarking on a search. The exceptions are the years 1923-1924, and some of those for 1919-1922, when an individual Form 30A was used. If a passenger was born or died at sea, there is usually a notation on the passenger list beside the name. There are no separate series of records relating to births and deaths at sea.

Lists of passengers on Hudson's Bay Company ships are to be found in their log books already mentioned – *see* page 26.

**India:** Lists of both inward and outward passengers are to be found in the log books of East Indiamen already mentioned – *see* page 26. Earlier passenger lists may be found in the *East India Company Letter Books, 1625-1753: E/3/84-111* in the Oriental and India Office Collections at the British Library. A few log books of East Indiamen are to be found in *Section E. Private Records* of the Hudson's Bay Company Archives – *see* page 26.

**South Africa:** Passenger lists of ships arriving in, or passing through, South African ports have not been systematically kept and those that have survived are widely dispersed. For passengers who travelled from Germany in the 19th century they have been published.[63] Some other shipping lists have been published, but they are fragmentary - a few transcripts may be found on the web and a useful starting point is www.genealogy.co.za/passengers.htm. *South Africa* magazine, published in London, is a useful source for those who emigrated from the UK to Southern Africa in the period 1890-1925 - a full run is available at the British Library Newspaper Library. It includes lists of passengers embarking at British ports for South Africa, and those embarking at South African ports for the UK and sometimes elsewhere. It also contains announcements of births, marriages and deaths, but usually only for the richer members of society.

**New Zealand:** Two series of ships' papers held by Archives New Zealand may help.[64] The first relates to New Zealand Company ships bringing immigrants between 1839 and 1853 [NZC 36]; the second is a sequence of ships' papers created from the inward letters (1871-1888) of the Immigration Department [Im 5/4]. These give information about shipboard conditions and usually include a statement from the surgeon about births and deaths on board. From approximately 1883 to 1973, Archives New Zealand hold passenger lists for nearly all ships arriving in New Zealand in *Social Security Passenger Lists [SS series 1]*. Further details on these and other series may be found on their website www.archives.govt.nz/holdings/immigration.html.

**United States:** Numerous inward passenger lists survive for ships to the United States.[65] These may be broadly categorised as Customs Passenger Lists and Immigration Passenger Lists or Manifests.

*Original Customs Passenger Lists* (covering dates 1820-1920) include immigrants, tourists and returning US citizens. If an individual died en route then the date and circumstances should be recorded against his or her name. The master was also required to note details of any births on the voyage. *Copies and abstracts* of the original customs passenger lists (covering dates 1820-1905) were sent to the Secretary of State; these should contain the same information about passengers as given in the originals but some of it may be abbreviated. *State Department Transcripts* (covering dates 1819-1832) were made from the copies described above – these too contain information about deaths en route. This material forms part of the Records of the U.S. Customs Service, Record Group 36; most has been microfilmed.

The *Immigration Passenger Lists*, which start in 1882, also include immigrants, tourists and returning US citizens, but do not seem to have provision on the various types of form used for details of deaths en route. But, since they ask for every person's place of birth, they ought to record any births during the voyage. These form part of the Records of the Immigration and Naturalization Service, Record Group 85; the US National Archives has microfilm copies of these covering 1883-1945.

Although much indexing work has been, and continues to be, carried out on these records there is no one overall index to them;[*] but there is a useful guide on the web to available indexes.[66] So to make a successful search of these records it is, in general, necessary to know the port of arrival, the date of arrival and the ship's name.

**Medical Journals**

Although medical journals were required to be kept for specific categories of ship from quite early, very few of these seem to have survived. Two series, at TNA, contain medical journals from some emigrant, transport and convict ships. Series *Medical Journals (ADM 101)* contains those for convict ships (1817-1853), emigrant ships (1815-1853) and other selected journals (1785-1856) but it only comprises some 127 bundles of documents and so can only be a very small sample. The other series is *Surgeon Superintendents' Journals of Convict Ships (MT 32)*; it consist of a mere 12 volumes covering the period 1858-1867. Both series have indexes to the names of the ships within PROCAT – approximately 162 ships in all. It is also possible that other surgeons' logs may survive in archives overseas. For example it is known that some, mostly from the 1870s, are available at Archives New Zealand;[67] it would seem also as if newspapers of the time in New Zealand often printed these reports.[68]

These journals are usually indexed by patients' names and record details of the ailment, treatment and progress of recovery or otherwise; a lengthy account is quite usual. An example taken from the surgeon's journal of a convict ship is shown in Figure 8.

---

[*]   The nearest there is to this is the on-going multi-volume *Passenger and Immigration List Index* by P William Filby and Mary K Meyer (Gale Research Company: Detroit), published from 1981 onwards, but it only covers lists in print and not original records.

## Wreck reports

The requirement, under the Merchant Shipping Act 1854, to obtain details about vessels in distress on the coast of the United Kingdom has resulted in the filing of a number of documents. Examinations of Deponents (Forms Wr.2, 2a and 2b.) are to be found, amongst the various series of Customs Outport Records:

| Port | Depositions | |
|------|-------------|---|
| | dates | references |
| Ramsgate | 1891-1922 | CUST 52/104-111 |
| Exeter, Teignmouth, Brixham, Salcombe | 1861-1877, 1879-1886 | CUST 64/187-1888 |
| Plymouth | 1859-1866, 1869-1899, 1901-1922 | CUST 218-226 |
| Scilly Isles | 1878-1927 | CUST 68/178-181 |
| Lundy | 1868-1885 | CUST 69/168 |
| Bristol Channel Ports, Padstow, Appledore, Bideford, Barnstaple | 1886-1888 | CUST 69/230 |
| Preston, Heysham, Lancaster | 1869-1900, 1913-1925 | CUST 81/57, 59 |
| North Shields | 1884-1889, 1891-1922 | CUST 87/1001-104 |
| Stockton | 1860-1881 | CUST 89/156 |
| Whitby | 1906-1920 | CUST 90/73 |
| Scarborough | 1876-1921 | CUST 91/102-109 |
| Grimsby | 1900-1909 | CUST 94/142 |
| King's Lynn, Wells, Blakeney and Cley | 1884-1928 | CUST 96/122-124 |
| Colchester | 1876-1881, 1892-1899 | CUST 100/104-105 |
| Maldon, Bradwell, Burnham | 1876-1881 | CUST 101/94 |
| Newport | 1868-1909 | CUST 71/131-137 |
| Cardiff | 1861-1870 | CUST 72/250-255 |
| Aberystwyth | 1868-1921 | CUST 76/100-102 |
| Bangor | 1880-1923 | CUST 78/197-199 |
| Isle of Man | 1859-1930, 1944-1970 | CUST 104/231-233, 277, 297-298 |

Letter books for some of these ports, as well as others, are available; these might record additional details but significant searching would be needed to uncover anything.

The regulations were broadly interpreted and applied not just to the loss of, or damage to, the vessel but also covered instances where simply some of the cargo was lost in a bad storm. Sometimes the events described took place some distance from the coast of the UK: in one instance five days out of Liverpool bound for Montevideo. The books containing the depositions are indexed by both the ship's name and that of the deponent.

The standard form on which a deposition was recorded provides for details of the incident and, under item 16, details of any loss of life. Only in rare instances are names recorded but the other records described in this book should allow them to be deduced. An example taken from the examination of James L Tweedie, by the Receiver of Wreck at the Port of Ramsey, Isle of Man, concerning the stranding of the *Caradoc* of Glasgow, of which he was mate, in January 1868 (CUST 104/231 p.178) reads:

---

16. Particulars of lives lost and saved:

    16. That in consequence of the *Stranding* —— the said Ship *One* life was lost by *Drowning* —— the remainder *Six* —— in all being saved by *the hawser and were all landed by about five P.M., that a little time after they had landed they were told, that a messenger had been sent for a Rocket Apparatus, but that it was in use at another vessel, that deponent was taken for shelter to a house near the place, and at about 9 PM the Agent for Lloyds came there.*

        *The Master Robert Donaldson has left a widow and three children – residing Eaglesfield Street Maryport Cumberland*

---

There is a wide range of other records relating to the loss of merchant ships, both in times of peace and war. Some useful sources are referred to in the standard works[69] and in TNA's leaflet.[70]

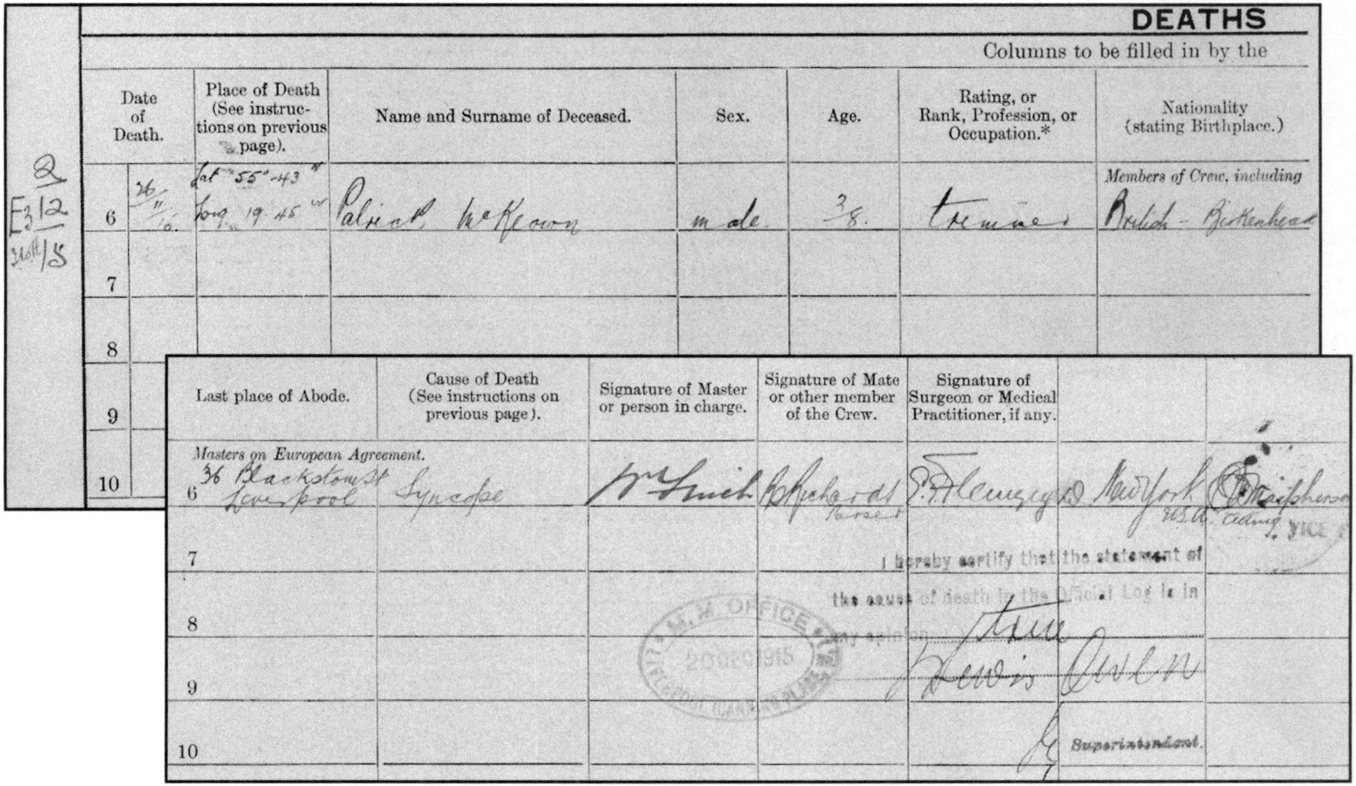

**DEATHS**

Columns to be filled in by the

| | Date of Death. | Place of Death (See instructions on previous page). | Name and Surname of Deceased. | Sex. | Age. | Rating, or Rank, Profession, or Occupation.* | Nationality (stating Birthplace.) |
|---|---|---|---|---|---|---|---|
| | | | | | | | *Members of Crew, including* |
| 6 | 26/11/15 | Lat 55°-43" N Long 19-45" W | Patrick McKeown | male | 38 | Fireman | British - Birkenhead |
| 7 | | | | | | | |
| 8 | | | | | | | |
| 9 | | | | | | | |
| 10 | | | | | | | |

| | Last place of Abode. | Cause of Death (See instructions on previous page). | Signature of Master or person in charge. | Signature of Mate or other member of the Crew. | Signature of Surgeon or Medical Practitioner, if any. | | |
|---|---|---|---|---|---|---|---|
| | *Masters on European Agreement.* | | | | | | |
| 6 | 36 Blackstone St Liverpool | Syncope | Wm Finch | B. Richards Purser | E. Fleming | New York | |
| 7 | | | | | | | |
| 8 | | | | | | | |
| 9 | | | | | | | |
| 10 | | | | | | | |

I hereby certify that the statement of the cause of death in the Official Log is in my opinion true

Lewis Owen

Superintendent.

M.M. OFFICE 20 DEC 1915 LIVERPOOL

*Figure 1: Death entry from the tabular section of a merchant ship's logbook:* Adriatic *(ON 124061), 25 November to 17 December 1915 (PRO BT 165/1200)*

34

## OFFICIAL LOG of the
### from                                   towards

| Date of the Occurrence entered with Hour. | Place of the Occurrence, or situation by Latitude and Longitude at Sea. | Date of Entry. | Entries required by Act of Parliament. | Amount of Fine or Forfeiture Inflicted. |
|---|---|---|---|---|
| 4 pm. 26/11/15 | at sea Lat. 55-43" Long 19.45" | 26/11/15 | Patrick McKeown, trimmer 173. died suddenly in stokehold from syncope and fatty degeneration of heart. W Finch Master J Richardson Ch Engineer S F Fleming M.D Doctor | |
| 11 am. 27/11/15 | Lat. 55.08" Long 21.38" | 27/11/15 | The body of Patrick McKeown, trimmer 173. was committed to the deep and a church of England burial service held. Ch Off W Finch Master J Richardson Ch Engineer S F Fleming M.D Doctor | |

*Figure 2: Death and burial details from the narrative section of a merchant ship's logbook:* Adriatic *(ON 124061), 25 November to 17 December 1915 (PRO BT 165/1200)*

41

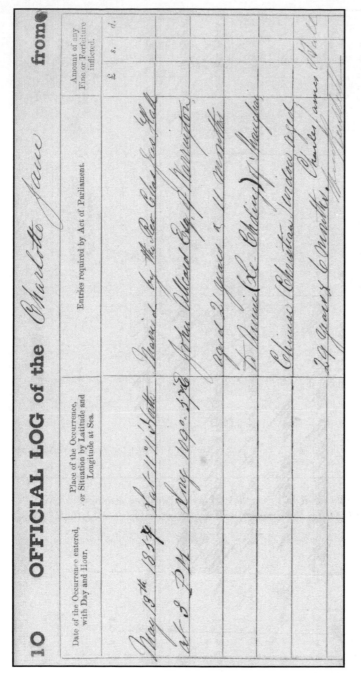

Figure 3: Marriage entry from the narrative section of merchant ship's log book: Charlotte Jane, 1857 (PRO BT 165/2035)

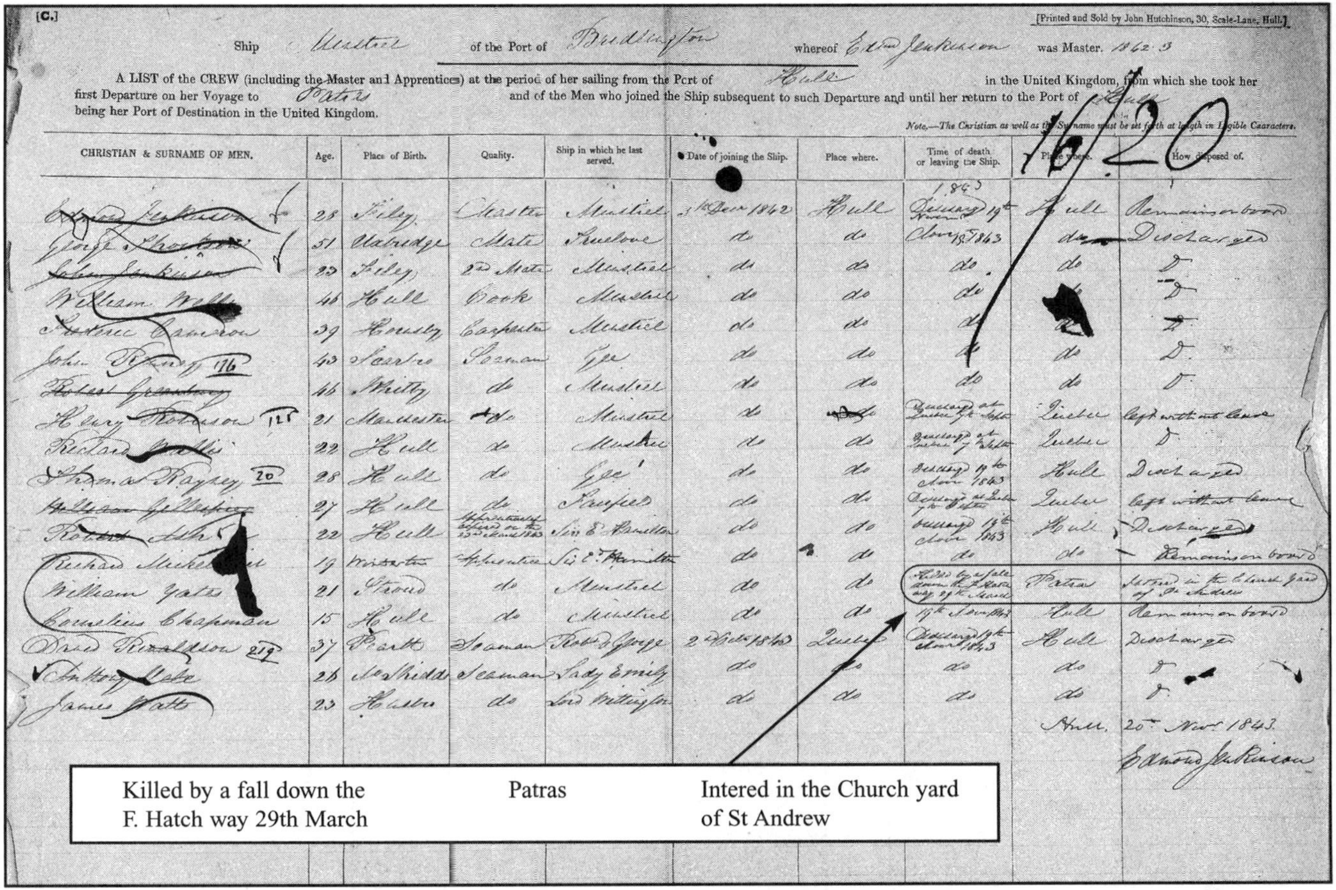

Figure 4: Death of a crew member from a crew list: Minstrel of Bridlington, 1843. (PRO BT 98/184)

PARTICULARS OF ALL BIRTHS AND DEATHS * OF PERSONS OTHER THAN THE CREW
PURSUANT TO SEC. 273 OF "THE MERCHANT

* NOTE.—When the deceased is a Member of the Crew the particu

BIRTHS.

| Names and Descriptions of Parents. | Date of Child's Birth. | Sex of Child. | Christian Name given to Child. | When given. | By whom Christened. |
|---|---|---|---|---|---|
| Wm & Mary Ryan | 29/11/65 | Male | | | |
| Martin & Ann Lee | 3/12/65 | Do | | | |
| Jacob & Hannah Hatfield | 10/10/66 | Do | John | | not yet christened J. M. H. |

AND OF ALL MARRIAGES THAT HAVE OCCURRED ON BOARD DURING THE VOYAGE;
SHIPPING ACT, 1854," 17 & 18 VICT. CAP. 104.

ers are to be inserted in the proper columns on the other side.

DEATHS.

| Name and Description of Deceased. | Sex. | Age. | Place of Birth. | Cause of Death. | Date of Death. |
|---|---|---|---|---|---|
| Bridget Lee | Female | 1½ | Ireland | Atrophy | 26/12/65 |
| Alexander Fraser | Male | 2 | Scotland | Peritonitis | 16/1/66 |
| Thomas Ryan | do | 26 | Ireland | Phthisis | 4/2/66 |
| David Mulholland | do | 18 | do | do | 17/2/66 |
| Ann McGovern | Female | 21 | do | Dysentery | 22/2/66 |

*Figure 5: Birth and death entries from a merchant ship's crew list:*
Africana *(ON 37160) 1867 (PRO BT 99/368)*

Name of Ship  Arabia        Official Number  105587

## RETURN OF BIRTHS.

| Date of Birth. | Name (if any) of Child | Sex. | Name and Surname of Father. | Rank, Profession, or Occupation of Father. | Name and Surname of Mother. | Maiden Surname of Mother. | Father. Nationality (stating Birthplace). | Last Place of Abode. | Mother. Nationality (stating Birthplace). | Last Place of Abode. |
|---|---|---|---|---|---|---|---|---|---|---|

## RETURN OF DEATHS.

| Date of Death. | Place of Death. | Name and Surname of Deceased. | Rating, or Rank, Profession, or Occupation. | Age. | Sex. | Nationality (stating Birthplace). | Last Place of Abode. | Cause of Death. |
|---|---|---|---|---|---|---|---|---|
| | | | Masters, on European Agreement. including Members of Crew. | | | | | |
| 6/11/16 | At Sea | R.P. Orme | Asst. Engineer | 23 | Male | British | Southampton { 145 Alma Rd Southampton } | Ship foundered |
| 6. do | -do | F. Grainger | do | 27 | do | | Carlisle { Southerfield Aikton, Carlisle } | do |

Members of Crew, Lascars and others, on Asiatic Agreement.

9 members of native Crew (Engine Dept.) names unknown

whom wire to handed to Bombay as soon as may be.

Persons who were not Members of the Crew (including Pilgrims, Coolies, etc.)

M.M OFFICE
23 NOV 1916
DOCK STREET E

[P.T.O.]

Figure 6: Entries from the B&D1 list filed by the Arabia (ON 105587) in November 1916.
© Crown Copyright, 2003, National Maritime Museum, London

45

## * BIRTHS ON THE VOYAGE.

| NAME OF INFANT. | WHETHER MALE OR FEMALE. | NAMES OF PARENTS. | NATIONALITY. |
|---|---|---|---|
| Unnamed | Male | Mr Antonio Valente de Mattos. Mrs Paula Correa de Mattos. | Portaguze |

## * DEATHS ON THE VOYAGE.

| NAME. | WHETHER MALE OR FEMALE. | AGE | OCCUPATION. | NATIONALITY. | CAUSE OF DEATH. |
|---|---|---|---|---|---|
| Unnamed | Male. | 2 hours. | — | Portaguze | Acathenia or Premature birth |

\* There is also a separate Return of Births and Deaths to be filled up by the Master and sent to the Registrar-General of Seamen, under a Penalty of £5. (*See* Sec. 254 of the Merchant Shipping Act, 1894.)

*Figure 7:  Birth and death entries recorded in the passenger list of the Avon (ON 124665), belonging to the Royal Mail Steam Packet Company, arriving at the port of Southampton from Buenos Aires. April 1920 (PRO BT 26/683)*

46

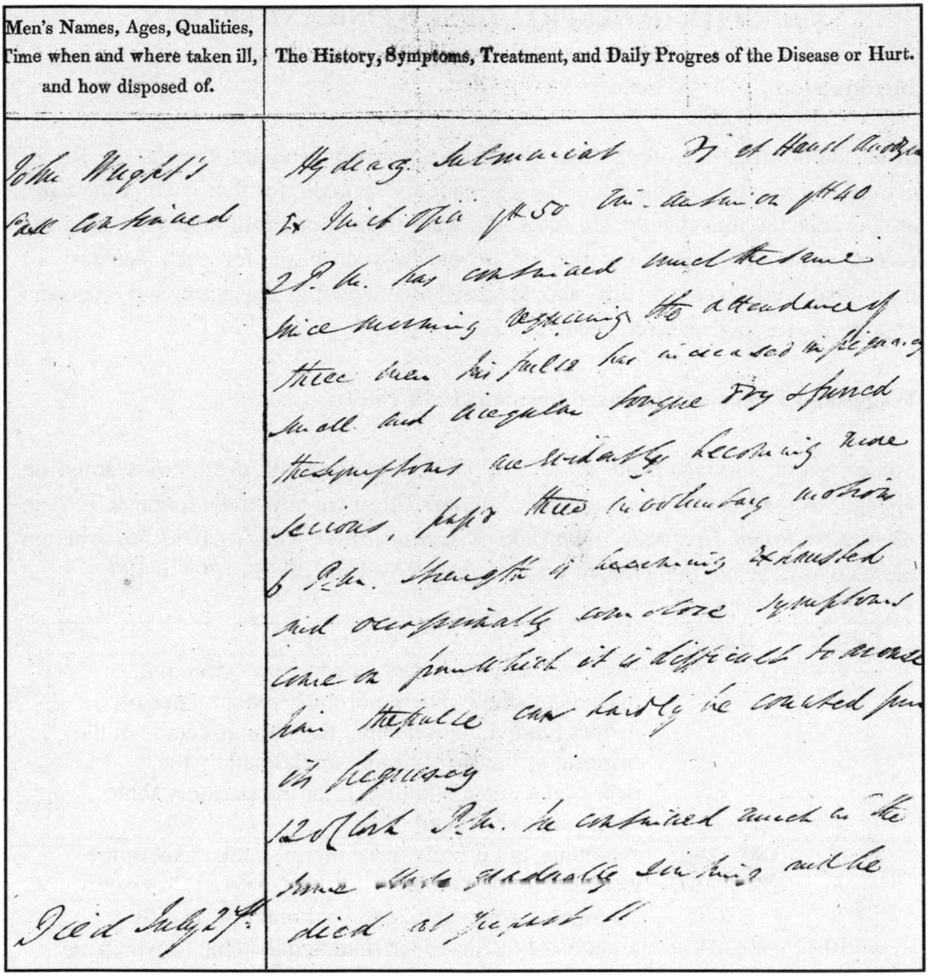

| Men's Names, Ages, Qualities, Time when and where taken ill, and how disposed of. | The History, Symptoms, Treatment, and Daily Progres of the Disease or Hurt. |
|---|---|
| John Wright's Case continued | Hydrarg. Submuriat. [illegible] of [illegible] Ex Tinct Opii gtt 50 [illegible] gtt 40 |
| | 2 P.M. has continued much the same since morning requiring the attendance of three men his pulse has increased in frequency small and irregular tongue dry & furred the symptoms are evidently becoming more serious, pass[d] three involuntary motions |
| | 6 P.M. strength is becoming exhausted and occasionally convulsive symptoms come on from which it is difficult to arouse him the pulse can hardly be counted from its frequency |
| | 12 o'Clock P.M. he continued much in the same [illegible] gradually sinking and he |
| Died July 27th | died at [illegible] 11 |

*Figure 8: Extract from the Surgeon's Journal of the convict ship* Lady Nugent, *1837 (PRO ADM 101/41/8)*

# REGISTRAR-GENERAL OF SHIPPING AND SEAMEN

## Introduction

From the information filed, mostly by the masters of merchant vessels, the RGSS compiled a number of registers. These secondary sources, for that is what they are, are described in this chapter. In Appendix 2 are to be found four tables detailing the record series, and piece number, on a year-by-year basis for each category of individual and event – this should assist in locating the surviving registers appropriate to your research needs.

## Wages and Effects of Deceased Seamen (1798-1889)

Some records survive, from the Act of 1797, recording the deaths of seamen on voyages from Great Britain to the West Indies. These are now to be found at TNA in *Admiralty: Royal Hospital Greenwich: Miscellaneous Records (ADM 80)* wherein pieces 6 to 12 relate to merchant seamen: these cover the period 1798 to 1831.

| Piece | Dates | Content |
|-------|-------|---------|
| 6 | 1798-1801 | Lists of monies received, at each port, from the masters of ships. These normally record dates of death of individual seamen. Sometimes details of the disposal of funds remaining unclaimed by the deceased seamen's family, after the statutory three years, are to be found. |
| 7 | 1803-1807 | Accounts, but usually these mention the name of the |
| 8 | 1806-1807 | deceased or his executor. |
| 9 | 1807 | Accounts, arranged by port, but making specific |
| 10 | 1808-1811 | mention of the deceased man and the ship to which he belonged. Date of death is not usually given. |
| 11 | 1829-1834 | Lists of monies received, at each port, from the |
| 12 | 1830-1831 | masters of ships. These normally record dates of death of individual seamen. Sometimes details of the disposal of funds remaining unclaimed by the deceased seamen's families, after the statutory three years, are to be found. |

Nothing seems to have survived, except on the crew lists themselves described earlier, as a consequence of an Act of 1834 whereby masters were required to keep a record of the effects left by, and wages due to, deceased seamen. The material surviving centrally dates from October 1851 when the Mercantile Marine Act 1850 came into force.

Information extracted or derived from crew lists, log books and wages and effects forms was transferred to a set of *Registers of Wages and Effects of Deceased Seamen (BT 153)*. These survive at TNA and cover the periods 1852-1881 and 1888-1889 with some late recordings up to 1893; the register covering the period April 1881 to May 1888 has not survived. In them is recorded:

- name and register ticket number of the deceased seaman
- date of engagement
- place, date and cause of death
- name and port of registry of ship

- master's name
- date and place of payment of wages
- amount of wages and date of receipt by the Board of Trade

- from 1866 they also record the seaman's age, his rating, and the ship's official number with a note of its voyages.

An example is shown in Figure 9.

There are two indexes to these registers in BT 154 (by seaman's name) and BT 155 (by ship's name) that provide page numbers within the registers in BT 153.

For those with an interest in Australia the series *Records of Deceased Seamen's Effects, 1913-1928,* in BP 219/3; preserved at the Queensland Regional Office of the National Archives of Australia, may be of interest;[71] these relate to the port of Maryborough.

**Registers of Births and Deaths at Sea**

*Introduction*
The registers compiled by the RGSS fall into three main categories: seamen, passengers, and British nationals (though the last does in fact cover those of other nationalities) – these are described below.

*Seamen: Deaths (1886-1890)*
For the period 1886-1890 there is a chronologically arranged series of registers, *Monthly Lists of Deceased Seamen (BT 156)* that record:

- name, age and rating of deceased seaman
- nationality or birthplace, and last address

- cause and place of death
- ship's name, official number and port of registry

In addition there is a series of *Registers of Seamen's Deaths Classified by Cause (BT 157)*. They record, according to type of illness or disease, accidents of various kinds or indeed murder:

- Class of Disease &c.
- Vessel: name; official number; port of registry; UK, Colonial or Fishing; tonnage
- Owner

- Deceased: date of death; name; age; rating; cause of death; place of death
- Voyage from and to
- Remarks

This last series should not be ignored as it may reveal some surprises. Whilst looking for an individual who had purportedly been murdered at sea, we came across the entry for the *Young Dick*, a sailing vessel registered in Wellington, New Zealand, captained by J H Rodgers with 14 crew and 118 passengers (BT 157/8 fo.274). It had sailed from Maryborough, Queensland to the South Sea Islands, in the labour trade in July 1886 — but had not made it, as can be seen from the remarks shown in Figure 10.

*Passengers: Births (1854-1889) and Deaths (1854-1890)*
*Registers of Births, Deaths and Marriages of Passengers at Sea (BT 158)* contain details of births, deaths and marriages of passengers taken from ships' official log books for the following periods: births (1854-1889), deaths (1854-1890) and marriages (1854-1883). These records do not seem to cover foreign-registered ships, or include foreign nationals, even after 1874 – *see* next section. There is an index to births and deaths from 1872 to 1890.

Scanned images of this series, together with an index, are available on-line at www.nationalarchivist.com. Their claim though that the records relate to more than just passengers does perhaps need further scrutiny as the examples given all seem to relate to individuals who were not members of the crew, for instance a birth to the master's wife or death of a master (who is technically not crew). But their point that searching these records may be overlooked if too narrow an interpretation is placed on their description is well-founded.

The information given in the registers is:

| BIRTH DETAILS | DEATH DETAILS |
|---|---|
| • name and description of parents | • name, sex, age, rank, profession or occupation, and nationality or birthplace of the deceased |
| • date of child's birth | |
| • sex of child | |
| • Christian name given to child | • last place of abode |
| • When given | • date, place and cause of death |
| • by whom christened | • ship's name, official number and port of registry and trade |
| • ship's name and official number | |
| • date of filing | |

An example from a birth register is shown in Figure 11.

*'British Nationals': Births (1875-1888) and Deaths (1875-1891)*
From 1874, the RGSS was required to report births and deaths at sea, aboard all ships registered in Britain or its colonies and on foreign-registered ships carrying passengers to or from the UK, to the Registrars General of England and Wales, Scotland and Ireland (the General Register Offices). These are to be found in the series *Registers of Birth at Sea of British Nationals, 1875-1891, (BT 160)* and *Registers of Deaths at Sea of British Nationals 1875-1888 (BT 159)*. The names of these series are misleading[*] as they include events related to persons of any

---

[*] The forms which comprise these volumes are entitled "Returns of Births/Deaths at Sea reported to the Registrar General of Shipping and Seamen under the Merchant Shipping Act 1854 and the Births and Deaths Registration Act 1874". The later Act specifically, in section 37, covers foreign nationals and foreign-registered ships travelling to or from an UK port.

nationality, not just British nationals. They should also cover events on foreign-registered passenger ships travelling to or from an UK port, but there is little evidence of this in the registers themselves.

There are separate volumes for England, Scotland and Ireland corresponding to the GRO to which the details were to be reported. The registers for Scotland and Ireland contain details where the deceased, or the father of the child (or mother if it was a bastard), was a 'Scotch or Irish subject of Her Majesty'. The registers for England include all events not reported to the GROs for Scotland and Ireland and thus contain entries for foreign nationals as well as those for English and Welsh subjects.

The information given in the registers is:

| BIRTH DETAILS | DEATH DETAILS |
|---|---|
| • name and number of the ship<br>• date of ship's arrival in port<br>• date of birth<br>• name and sex of child<br>• name and occupation of father<br>• maiden name of mother<br>• parents' nationalities and last place of residence | • details of the ship<br>• date and cause of death<br>• name, sex, age, occupation, nationality and last address of deceased<br>• whether deceased was passenger or crew |

An example from a register of deaths reported to the GRO (Dublin) is shown in Figure 12.

*1891 onwards*
From 1891 a new series of registers was introduced that combined records of the births, deaths and marriages of passengers at sea and the records of deaths and marriages of seamen at sea. The registers are at TNA in PRO series *Registers and Indexes of Births, Marriages and Deaths of Passengers and Seamen at Sea (BT 334)*. The covering dates and information given in these registers is as follows:

## BIRTHS (1891-1960):

- name of ship, official number and port of registry - an X against the name indicating a sailing ship
- date of birth, name, sex of child
- name of father, rank or profession or occupation
- name of mother, maiden surname of mother
- father's nationality/birthplace and last place of abode
- mother's nationality/birthplace and last place of abode

## DEATHS (1891-1964):

- name of ship, official number, port of registry and trade [*see* Appx 3]
- date, place and cause of death,
- name of deceased, sex, age, rating [for seamen, an * indicates an Asiatic serving under an Asiatic Agreement], rank or profession or occupation [for non-seamen]
- nationality or birthplace, last place of abode

*Note:* deaths of current and former crew members taking place ashore, for instance in hospital, were required to be recorded wherever possible in addition to those that occurred actually at sea.

There is also a column, in most of these registers entitled 'Which RG has been informed'. It should be noted that, although the RGSS was required to report deaths to the appropriate General Register Office, over half of the entries on some pages are blank in that column. It has been suggested that where there was no first-hand evidence of the loss of the vessel, or if a person was presumed lost overboard but there was no eye-witness to the event, then in these circumstances an entry might have been made in the RGSS's registers but that the evidence was insufficient to support a return to the GRO. Also in some cases when the death actually took place ashore then details may again not have been forwarded – but the precise rules are not now clear. Care also needs to be taken in interpreting the 'Which RG has been informed' column since either the abbreviations E (for England), S (for Scotland), I for (Ireland) and NI (for Northern Ireland after 1922) or alternatively L (for London), E (for Edinburgh) and D (for Dublin) may have been used. But the context will soon tell you whether E means England or Edinburgh.

A further column, entitled 'Source of information', indicates from which document(s) the record has been extracted. There is a wide variety of crew lists, log books, births and deaths reports, wages and effects and inquiry report forms that could be being referred to. Not all of these have survived and those that have are not necessarily in unique document series. The previous chapter contains a description of what now survives. The abbreviations given in this column should guide you as to where to look next for the primary source referred to. The list below, although incomplete, may assist:

| Abbreviation[#] | Refers to: | Search next in: |
|---|---|---|
| LB | Log book (*see* note) | ⎫ |
| O# | Official Log | ⎬ Log books |
| | | ⎭ |
| D&O# | Official Log and Crew List | ⎫ |
| Eng# | Agreement and Crew List | ⎬ Crew lists and log books ⎭ |
| C&D | Casualty & Deaths list | Casualty & Death lists or Crew lists |
| 1 or I | Return of Births & Deaths (B&D1) | ⎫ |
| W&E1 | Wages and Effects of Deceased Seamen | ⎬ Returns of Births & Deaths |
| CC15 or C15 | Report relating to wages and effects of deceased seamen | ⎭ |
| 3 | Report relating to deaths (B&D3) | Inquiries into deaths at sea |
| RG | Registrar General's file reference | File of correspondence attached to Returns of Births & Deaths |

[#] where # may be any number

*Note:* Often one will find, in the last column, the number 1 followed by a manuscript addition of LB plus a fraction (e.g. 7/15). This indicates that the information was taken initially from a B&D1 form and that a log book was subsequently filed (in this case in July 1915).

These registers should cover all births and deaths aboard British-registered merchants ships, whatever the nationality of the individuals involved. They should also include information about these events occurring aboard any vessel, whatever its registry, carrying passengers to or from a UK port. But they ought not to include events aboard vessels registered in a British colony where the event occurs within the jurisdiction of that colony.

This series consists mostly of printed registers as described above; they are designated on the first page as GR160. An example taken from one of these is shown as Figure 13. There are in addition a few registers, designated as B&D16 and

B&D17, where the entries are in manuscript. These contain fewer entries than are found in the GR160 registers and just record those entries actually sent to one of the GROs. An example taken from one of these latter registers is shown as Figure 14.

The series includes index volumes for births (1891-1960) and deaths (1891-1964). These are arranged both by ships' names and by individuals' names.

Later registers of births and deaths at sea are held by the RSS; a request for information from them may attract a fee.

There were several copies made of the printed GR160 registers referred to above; they date from 1886. Copies of registers related to deaths of seamen are to be found at TNA, as already described, in BT 334 and, prior to 1891, in BT 156. But it is possible that other copies may be found. Some are held by the GRO for England and Wales at Southport; it is believed that the NMM may have some such registers and it is known that the Glasgow Room of the Mitchell Library, in Glasgow, holds 22 such volumes for deceased seamen covering the period 1886 to 1952.

For those with an interest in Australia the following series of records, preserved at the regional offices of the National Archives of Australia, may be of interest:[72]

| Register of Deaths at Sea, with an index 1868 *[sic]* to 1922 | 1893-1922, | South Australian office CRS D7 | Port Adelaide |
|---|---|---|---|
| Register of Seamen Engaged, Discharged, Died or Deserted | 1903-1942 1941-1946 | South Australian office AP 231/1 CRS D458 | Port Pirie |
| Register of Deaths and Accidents | from 1922 | Victorian office CRS B646 | Melbourne |

**World Wars 1 & 2**

If the death occurred as a result of a merchant vessel being sunk by an enemy submarine, then the Admiralty records may yield useful information. Many reports of such sinkings are to be found, for the period 1916-1918, in *Admiralty: Historical Section: Records used for Official History (ADM 137)* and PROCAT often lists these under the ship's name. Alternatively reference to the appropriate file may be found in *Admiralty: Digests and Indexes (ADM 12)* under the name of the ship and perhaps under the names of key individuals. Lists of British merchant vessels attacked by enemy submarines, with reports of actions and sinkings (1916-1918), are also to be found in *Admiralty: Station records: Plymouth Correspondence (ADM 131/113 to 118)*. Both these sets of files often name the casualties and those killed or lost as well as giving the circumstances.

The NMM holds a card index of deaths of merchant seamen during World War 2 (up to 1948). This source classifies deaths by cause according to a numerical code, the meaning of which is not now clear. An example is shown in Figure 15.

TNA holds, amongst the series *Registrar General of Shipping and Seamen: Rolls of Honour, Wars of 1914-1918 and 1939-1945 (BT 339)*, five volumes related to the deaths of merchant seamen during World War 2. Two volumes (BT 339/1-2) are arranged alphabetically by ships' names recording: the ship's name plus the name, rank or rating, and date of death of the seaman. Two more volumes (BT 339/3-4) are arranged by seamen's name recording rank or rating, age at death, address (town), date of death and name of ship. The final volume (BT 339/8) is a Roll of Honour for T124 (that is Fishing Trawler crews employed on minesweeping and patrolling duties on a named vessel for the duration of the war 1939-1945); this is arranged according to seamen's names. Despite its title, the series does not contain similar rolls for World War 1.

Papers on Royal Naval Reserve officers who were casualties, missing or prisoners of war, during World War 2, are in BT 164/23.

Those British merchant seaman who served, and perished, on US Navy ships during World War 2 may be listed in a US Coast Guard publication.[73] The names of British merchant seaman have been extracted from this and published on the web at http://mnrollofhonour.com/[*]

---

[*] There are sufficient errors in the description of this material to make us a little cautious about the accuracy of the transcript itself.

## Registers of Marriage at Sea

Details of marriages performed aboard British merchant vessels were extracted from the log books and entered by the RGSS into registers. Those between 1858 and 1883 are recorded along with births and deaths in *Registers of Births, Deaths and Marriages of Passengers at Sea (BT 158)*. Table 6 in Appendix 2 lists the relevant piece numbers.

Scanned images of this series, together with an index, are available on-line at www.nationalarchivist.com. Their claim though that the records relate to more than just passengers does perhaps need further scrutiny as the examples given all seem to relate to individuals who were not members of the crew, for example the marriage of the master – his bride was unlikely to be a crew member. But their point that searching these records may be overlooked if too narrow an interpretation is placed on their description is well-founded.

It seems that these entries, along with subsequent later additions, are found in *Registers and Indexes of Births, Marriages and Deaths of Passengers and Seamen at Sea (BT 334)*. BT 334/117 is the volume reference covering marriages from 1854-1972; an example from these registers is shown in Figure 16. Later registers are with the RSS.

There is an integral index in BT 334/117. In addition a transcript of the 219 entries to be found in these two series has been compiled by Debbie Beavis and is available on the internet at www.theshipslist.com/Forms/marriagesatsea.html.

**Supporting material**

Within *Precedent Books, Establishment Papers etc (BT 167)* are a number of files that may assist in particular instances; such as:

| Reference | Description | Covering dates |
|---|---|---|
| BT 167/72 | Suicides: correspondence, reports and statistics | 1889-1907 |
| BT 167/73 | Suicides and deaths: statistics and summary of reports | 1891-1907 |
| BT 167/121 | Register of deaths of firemen and trimmers: gives ship's name, owner's name, nationality and rating of deceased, number of firemen and trimmers, coal consumption, relative severity of work on board the | December 1912 to 1925 |
| BT 167/122 | ship, temperature at the time of occurrence, date of occurrence, number of days on board before occurrence, locality of ship at the time, and when and where deceased joined the ship | 1925 to December 1940 |

Whilst these registers do not record the name of the deceased, this can usually be deduced from the other death registers and records. So if you are looking for details of the death of a fireman or trimmer, then these records should tell you the conditions under which he worked and died. Each volume contains an index to ships' names. An example is shown in Figure 17.

**Items reported to local officials**

One register of deaths and births at sea, first reported at Falmouth (1892-1918), is to be found amongst the Customs records in CUST 67/74. The reason for the compilation of this register is unclear and it is possible that others may still await discovery.

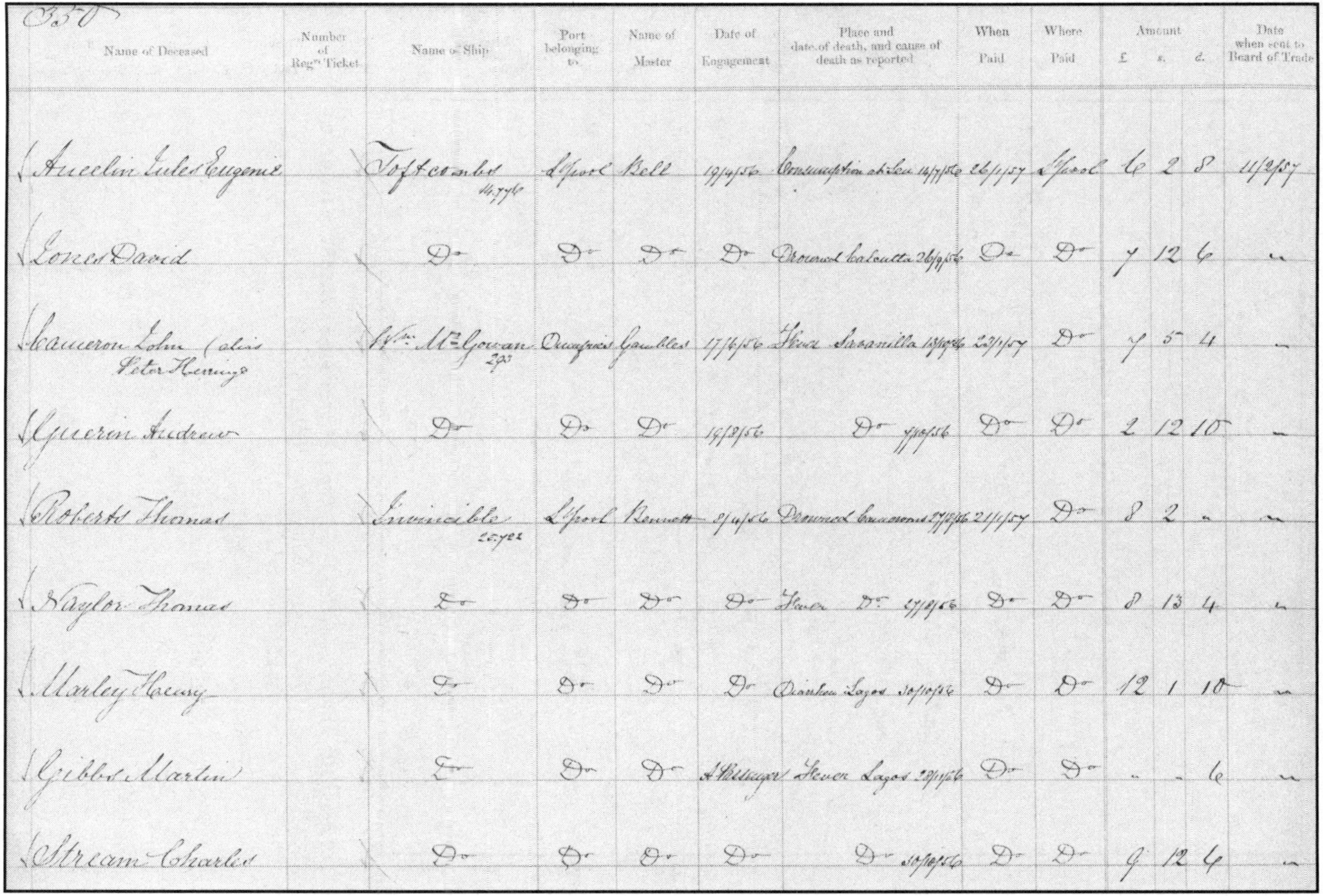

| Name of Deceased | Number of Regr. Ticket | Name of Ship | Port belonging to | Name of Master | Date of Engagement | Place and date of death, and cause of death as reported | When Paid | Where Paid | Amount £ | s. | d. | Date when sent to Board of Trade |
|---|---|---|---|---|---|---|---|---|---|---|---|---|
| Ancelin Jules Eugenie | | Tof+combe 14.774 | L'pool | Bell | 19/4/56 | Consumption at Sea 14/7/56 | 26/1/57 | L'pool | 6 | 2 | 8 | 11/2/57 |
| Jones David | | Do | Do | Do | Do | Drowned Calcutta 26/9/56 | Do | Do | 7 | 12 | 6 | " |
| Cameron John (alias Peter Herring) | | Wm. McGowan 293 | Dumfries | Gambles | 17/6/56 | Fever Sacramilla 13/10/56 | 27/1/57 | Do | 7 | 5 | 4 | " |
| Guerin Andrew | | Do | Do | Do | 19/8/56 | Do 4/10/56 | Do | Do | 2 | 12 | 10 | " |
| Roberts Thomas | | Invincible 25.722 | L'pool | Bennett | 8/4/56 | Drowned Cameroons 17/8/56 | 21/1/57 | Do | 8 | 2 | " | " |
| Naylor Thomas | | Do | Do | Do | Do | Fever Do 17/8/56 | Do | Do | 8 | 13 | 4 | " |
| Marley Henry | | Do | Do | Do | Do | Diarrhea Lagos 30/10/56 | Do | Do | 12 | 1 | 10 | " |
| Gibbs Martin | | Do | Do | Do | A Villager | Fever Lagos 29/11/56 | Do | Do | " | " | 6 | " |
| Stream Charles | | Do | Do | Do | Do | Do 30/10/56 | Do | Do | 9 | 12 | 4 | " |

Figure 9: *Register of Wages and Effects of Deceased Seamen, 1856 (PRO BT 153/2)*

Vessel missing – supposed to
have struck on Harrier Reef, Queens?

By paragraf in Shipping Gazette of 9.2.87
a letter dated Apia
Navigators Island 15.12.86.
A number of Melanesian Labourers
on their way home to Malaita, Soloman Group
have eaten up the entire crew of the
Ship & plundered the vessel –
The Capt & mate were residents of Apia
the crew consisted of Patagonians &
other Polynesians.

Supposed to refer to the previous
voyage –

*Figure 10: Murder recorded in the Register of Seamen's Deaths, classified by Cause, July 1886 (PRO BT 157/8)*

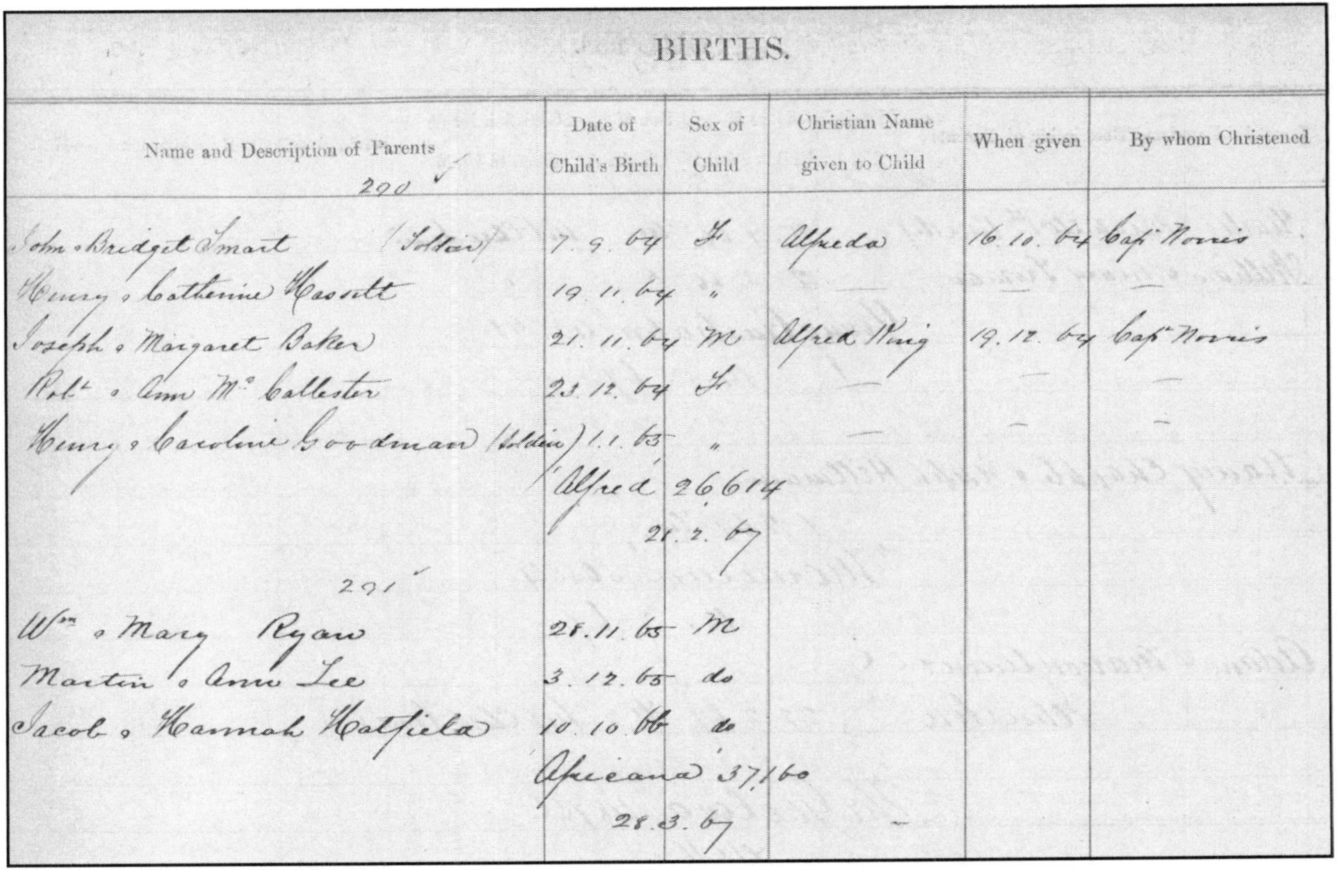

BIRTHS.

| Name and Description of Parents | Date of Child's Birth | Sex of Child | Christian Name given to Child | When given | By whom Christened |
|---|---|---|---|---|---|
| 290 | | | | | |
| John & Bridget Smart (Soldier) | 7. 9. 64 | F | Alfreda | 16. 10. 64 | Capt Norris |
| Henry & Catherine Hassett | 19. 11. 64 | " | — | — | — |
| Joseph & Margaret Baker | 21. 11. 64 | M | Alfred King | 19. 12. 64 | Capt Norris |
| Robt & Ann Mc Callester | 23. 12. 64 | F | — | — | — |
| Henry & Caroline Goodman (Soldier) | 1. 1. 65 | " | — | — | — |
| | 'Alfred' 26614 28. 2. 67 | | | | |
| 291 | | | | | |
| Wm & Mary Ryan | 28. 11. 65 | M | | | |
| Martin & Ann Lee | 3. 12. 65 | do | | | |
| Jacob & Hannah Hatfield | 10. 10. 66 | do | | | |
| | 'Africana' 37160 28. 3. 67 | | — | | |

*Figure 11: Birth entries from the Register of Births, Deaths and Marriages of Passengers at Sea, 1867 (PRO BT 158/3)*

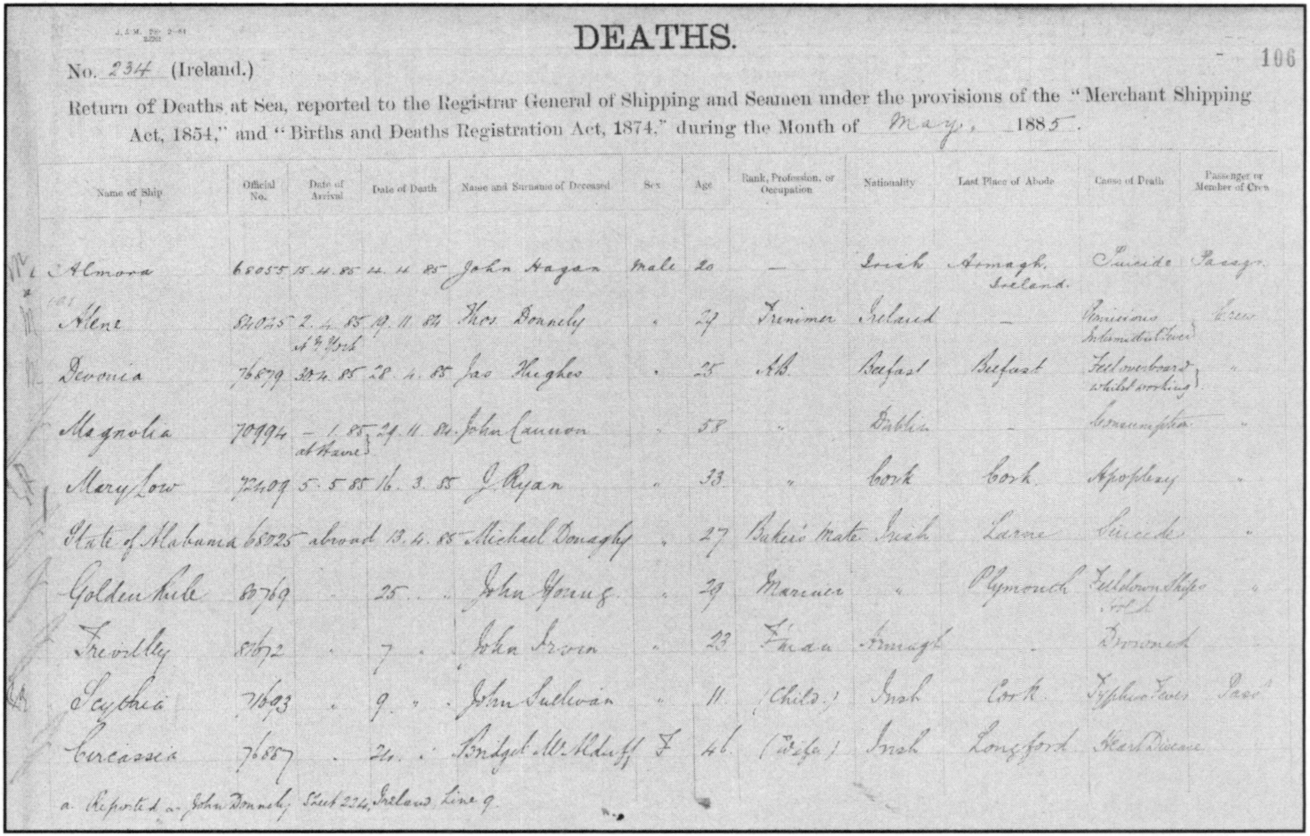

# DEATHS.

No. 234 (Ireland.) 106

Return of Deaths at Sea, reported to the Registrar General of Shipping and Seamen under the provisions of the "Merchant Shipping Act, 1854," and "Births and Deaths Registration Act, 1874," during the Month of May, 1885.

| Name of Ship | Official No. | Date of Arrival | Date of Death | Name and Surname of Deceased | Sex | Age | Rank, Profession, or Occupation | Nationality | Last Place of Abode | Cause of Death | Passenger or Member of Crew |
|---|---|---|---|---|---|---|---|---|---|---|---|
| Almora | 68055 | 15.4.85 | 4.4.85 | John Hagan | Male | 20 | — | Irish | Armagh, Ireland. | Suicide | Passgr. |
| Alene | 84025 | 2.4.85 at N York | 19.11.84 | Thos Donnely | " | 27 | Fireman | Ireland | — | Pernicious Intermittent Fever | Crew |
| Devonia | 76879 | 30.4.85 | 28.4.85 | Jas Hughes | " | 25 | A.B. | Belfast | Belfast | Fell overboard whilst working | " |
| Magnolia | 70994 | – 1.85 at Havre | 24.11.84 | John Cannon | " | 58 | " | Dublin | — | Consumption | " |
| Mary Low | 72409 | 5.5.85 | 16.3.85 | J. Ryan | " | 33 | " | Cork | Cork. | Apoplexy | " |
| State of Alabama | 68025 | abroad | 13.4.85 | Michael Donaghy | " | 27 | Baker's Mate | Irish | Larne | Suicide | " |
| Golden Rule | 80769 | " | 25 " | John Young | " | 29 | Mariner | " | Plymouth | Fell down Ships hold | " |
| Trevilley | 87672 | " | 7 " | John Irwin | " | 23 | Fireman | Armagh | — | Drowned | " |
| Scythia | 71693 | " | 9 " | John Sullivan | " | 11 | (Child) | Irish | Cork. | Typhoid Fever | Passr. |
| Circassia | 76887 | " | 21 " | Bridget McAlduff | F | 46 | (Wife) | Irish | Longford | Heart Disease | " |

a. Reported as John Donnely Sheet 224, Ireland Line 9.

*Figure 12: Death entries from the Register of Deaths of British Nationals: Ireland, May 1885 (PRO BT 159/7)*

| 1. Name and Surname. | 2. Age. | 3. Rank or Rating. | 4. Nationality or Birthplace. | 5. Last Place of Abode. | 6. Name. | 7. Official Number. | 8. Port of Registry. | 9. Net Tonnage. |
|---|---|---|---|---|---|---|---|---|
| Abdoo, Naif | 25 | Fireman* | Yemen | Aden | Grique | 115,933 | North Shields. | 2,099 |
| Allan, Archibald | 23 | Trimmer | Liverpool | 41, Cornwall St. | Gartshore | 81,969 | Liverpool | 966 |
| Arron, Aloysius | | | | | | | | |
| Aubrey, R. | | | | | | | | |
| Azis, Muckbool Ahamoo | | | | | | | | |
| Baker, J. H. | | | | | | | | |
| Barry, John | | | | | | | | |

Particulars of Death

| | 10. Date. | 11. Place. | 12. Cause. | 13. Remarks. | 14. Registrar General to whom the death has been reported. | 15. Official Reference. |
|---|---|---|---|---|---|---|
| | 16 Aug. 1914 | Bombay | Drowned | Engaged 25 June 1914 at Aden | E. | 1. £3 10/14 |
| | 23 Aug. 1914 | Hospital, Valencia | Typhoid | Discharged 5 Aug. 1914 | — | 1. |
| | 2 Sept. 1914 | At Sea | Missing | Engaged 26 Aug. 1914 at Colombo | E. | 1. £3 ./.. |
| | 19 July 1914 | At Sea | Cardiac failure | | E. | 1. £3 4/15 |
| | 20 July 1914 | At Sea | Accident | | E. | L. B. |
| | 18 Aug. 1914 | Delaware River | Missing | | E. | L. B. 1. |
| | 27 July 1914 | At Sea | Missing | | L | L. B. 1. |

Figure 13: *Deaths of seaman, from the Indexes and Registers of Births, Deaths and Marriages of Passengers and Seamen at Sea, September 1914 (PRO BT 334/62)*

# DEATHS.

B. & D. 17.

(5) (97907) Wt. 63xxx 500 5/0 W B & L

Return of Deaths at Sea, reported to the Registrar-General of Shipping and Seamen under the provisions of the "Merchant Shipping Act, 1894," during the month of *September* 1914.

| Name of Ship. | Official Number. | Date of Death. | Place of Death. | Name and Surname of Deceased. | Sex. | Age. | Rating or Rank Profession or Occupation. | Nationality (naming Birthplace). | Last Place of Abode. | Cause of Death. | Passenger or Member of Crew. |
|---|---|---|---|---|---|---|---|---|---|---|---|
| Mark Macdougall | 109184 | 19.7.14 during august island | At Sea lat. 29.48 N long 13.35 W | Abdorahon | Male | 25 | Fireman Interman | Bombay | Unknown | Gone overboard | Crew 1 / 1 |
| Burndyke | 92823 | 14th august | Bordeaux | Rahim Bux | Male | 43 | Interman | British Calcutta | W. Brunswickstt. So. Shields | Heart failure | do. 1 / 1 |
| Seindia | 112917 | 14th august | Marseilles | John Barron & Alfred Jackson | Male | 38 | Lascar | India | Bombay Balham Rd. | Congestion of lungs, Heart failure | do. 1 / 1 |
| Baltic | 118101 | 14th | New York | Robert Huggitt | Male | 30 | Steward | England | Antrim Riverford | Cerebral Haemorrhage | do. 1 / 1 |
| Maurani | 110697 | 31.7.14 | at sea | Amelia Opel | Male | 22 | Interman | Indian Bengali English | Calcutta | Heart failure | do. 1 / 1 |
| Campania | 102086 | Aug 22 | New York Steamboat | James Manon | Male | 50 | A.B. | English | Liverpool | Heart failure | do. 1 / 1 |
| Vina | 133529 | 11.8.14 | U.S.A | John P. Leary William | Male | 20 | Sailor | Liverpool British Galashiel | 33 Glendale Rd. Newcastle North Shields | drowned | do. 1 / 1 |
| Beaumont | 110381 | 30.8.14 | Savona | Johnson | Male | 48 | Interman Officers | Middle China | Wolverhampton St. | Fracture of skull | do. 1 / 1 |
| Graye | 118214 | 9.8.14 | Wadsworth | Lui Jit | Male | 20 | Boy | Canton East Indian | Hong Kong | Peritonitis | do. 1 / 1 |
| Elysia | 128221 | Aug 16.14 16th Aug. | N 61.7, 61.30 E | Mahdi M Ackden & Salmon A.H. | Male | 37 | Lascar Tindal | Rihai | Bombay Bromton | Cardiac failure | do. 1 / 1 |
| Royal Edward | 125650 | 1914 | Montreal | Abdul Hamid Ymi | Male | 36 | Trimmer | Budd | 1 Bromton 8 Paul Bristol | drowning | do. 1 / 1 |
| Gregory Apcar | 98305 | 11.3.14 3 hrs | Mexa lat. 16.24 S | Bundagally | Male | 30 | B R McJndl | Chittagong Indian | Calcutta | Bronchitis Nephritis | do. 1 / 1 |
| Assaye | 125285 | 5/8/14 5 p.m. & 8.30 pm | Kong 100.46 E | Francis M. Musla | Male | 38 | 2nd cook | Goona Indian | Bombay | Gallstung & Enteritis Scalding Suffocated Suicide | do. 1 / 1 |
| Goldenfield | | 1914 3 met | Manila | Jamralla Enchamalla | Male | 20 | Fireman | Indian Jullut | Calcutta | Jaundice | do. 1 / 1 |
| Nyanza | 123524 | 1914 | 36.48 N 57.11 W | Casoof Esmal | Male | 7 | Lascar | Banaun India | Saman India | Tubercle of Malaria, Wiringla Beliafa, Newfoundland | do. 1 / 1 |

*Figure 14: Deaths, from the Indexes and Registers of Births, Deaths and Marriages of Passengers and Seamen at Sea, reported to the GRO (England and Wales), September 1914 (PRO BT 334/63)*

CONDG | 362 | 531 | 663 | 3 | 39 | 42/12 | 383

| Nat. | Rank or Rating | Cause of Death | Ship | Age Group | Date of Death | R.of H List Number |
|---|---|---|---|---|---|---|
| | | | | | Res | |

Record of Death of Merchant Seaman

Surname: BROWN

Ship: *Accord*     Fishing

Other Names: Arnold Gordon

Official No: 145784

Address: Hut. 19, Site 4, R.A.F. Camp. Ellough, near Beccles.

Port of Registry: Peterhead

British/Fishing/Foreign

Birthplace: Geldeston     Country: England

Rank or Rating: Deck Hand

Date of Death: 8 Dec. 1947 Place of Death: At sea     Age at Death: 39

Cause of Death: Jumped off casing on to deck she gave a lurch and Brown disappeared overboard. Believed drowned

Register Entry:

Ppd. by: 296     Year: 1947     Month: December Page: 2

Ckd. by:

Reg. Gen.

G.R.     H

Figure 15: *Record of Death of Merchant Seaman: World War 2 Death cards*
© *Crown Copyright, 2003, National Maritime Museum, London*

| PARTICULARS OF SHIP. | | PARTICULARS CONCERNING MARRIAGE. | | | | | | | Source of Information. |
|---|---|---|---|---|---|---|---|---|---|
| Name | Official Number. | Date. | Christian and Surnames of both Parties. | Age | Whether Single, Widow, or Widower | Profession or Occupation. | Father's Christian and Surname. | Profession or Occupation of Father | |
| No. 6. Charlotte Jane | 26370 | 13 Mar. 1857 | John Allcard | 22 | – | – | – | – | |
| | | | Annie Le Gidday | 29½ | – | – | – | – | |
| | | | Married by Rev. C. James Hall | | | | | | |
| | | | William Russell – Master. | | | | | | |
| No. 7. Lillias | 24270 | 28 Sept. 1857 | Hy Harcourt Browning | 20 | – | – | – | – | |
| | | | Margaret Jones Payne | 20 | – | – | – | – | |
| | | | Married by Rev Storey | | | | | | |
| | | | William H. Bell – Mastr. | | | | | | |

*Figure 16: Marriages from the Indexes and Registers of Births, Deaths and Marriages of Passengers and Seamen at Sea, 1857 (PRO BT 334/117)*

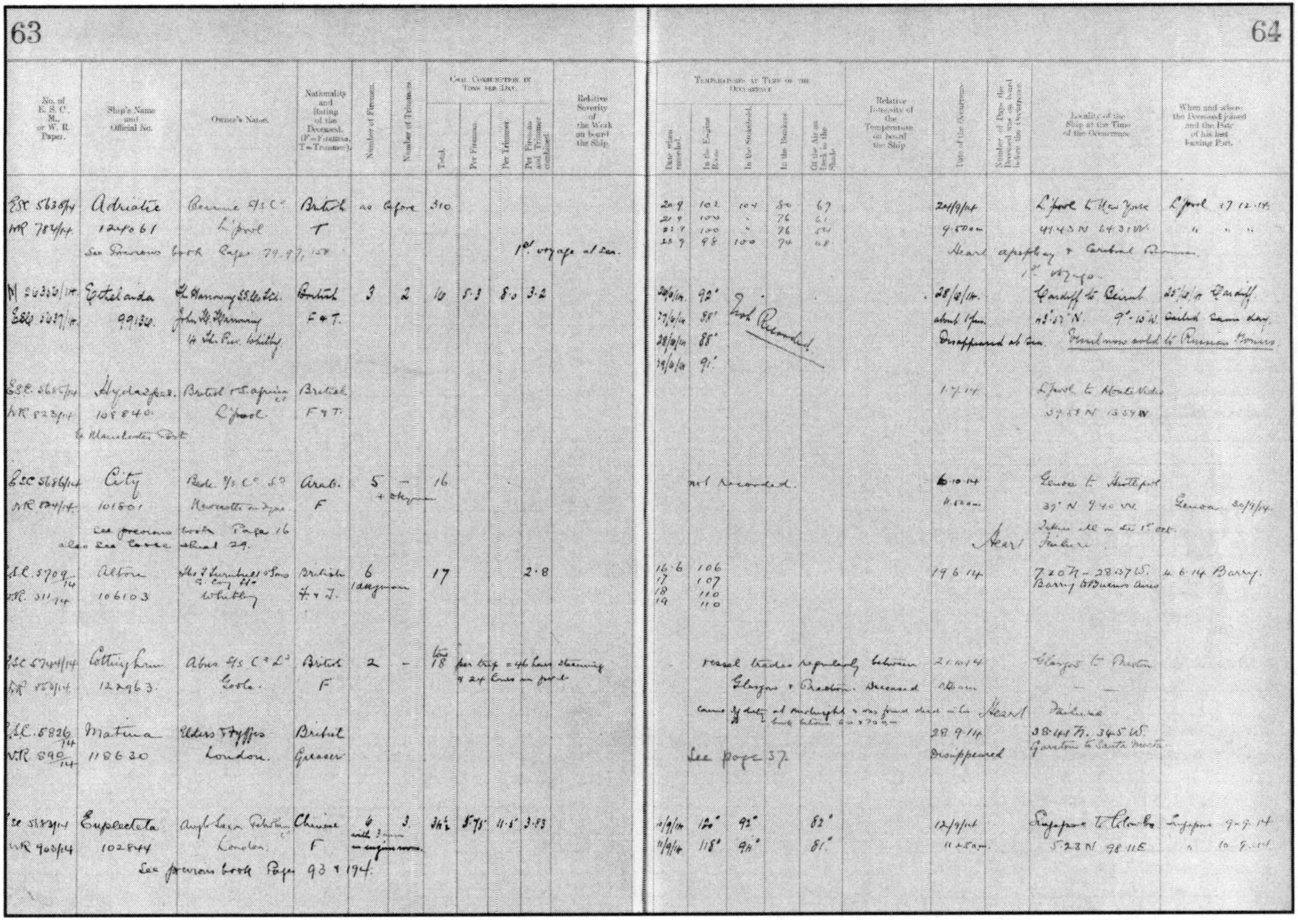

Figure 17: Register of Deaths of Firemen and Trimmers, 1914 (PRO BT 167/121)

# ROYAL NAVY

## Introduction

In the chapter on Legislation and Regulations we discovered just what records should have been created. Now we will look at just what has survived and over what period, what it contains, where it is to be found, and how it is arranged.

This chapter is concerned with primary sources related to events that occurred aboard Royal Navy ships. Later ones will discuss the secondary sources compiled by the Admiralty and by the General Register Offices. Two earlier chapters discussed the records related to merchant ships created by the vessel's master and by the RGSS.

Certain material mentioned in the chapter on Legislation and Regulations is known not to survive, and we may therefore dismiss any further consideration of it; namely:

- The certified copies of the minute, or log book entry, sent by the captain of a Royal Navy ship to the appropriate General Register Office survive probably only for Scotland. The log book should survive and the appropriate GRO's entry in the Marine Register survives but the certified copy referred to in the legislation does not survive except possibly for those sent to GRO (Scotland).*

## Log Books

The practice, in the Royal Navy, of keeping a log book recording events on board is long-standing going back at least to the 17th century. In fact several log books were made though not all have been preserved. These may conveniently be divided into the following categories:

- The **Rough Log** was kept hour by hour and signed by the officer of the watch on being relieved. These have not been officially preserved and any that survive do so by chance.

---

\* These are probably in the series of 'Intimations' at GRO (Scotland) - *see* pages 100 and 101.

- The **Captain's Log** contains daily navigational information (such as noon position and distance covered) together with a chronological summary of daily events recorded in the Rough Log. These logs were sent to the Admiralty and have been preserved at TNA in the series *Captains' Logs, 1669-1853 (ADM 51)*.

- The **Master's Log** contains detailed hourly navigational information (such as course steered, speed, wind direction) together with information about the ship's routine. Both the Master's and Captain's Logs were probably based on the Rough Log but included only the information that each man considered relevant - so they are not duplicates. These logs were sent to the Admiralty and have been preserved at TNA in the series *Masters' Logs, 1672-1840 (ADM 52)*.

- The **Lieutenant's Log** was kept by an officer of the ship. It contains navigational information and a journal of events but is usually briefer than either the Captain's or Master's Logs. These logs were sent to the Admiralty and have been preserved at the National Maritime Museum (1673-1809).

- The **Ship's Log** superseded those of the Captain and Master; they survive at TNA in the series *Ships' Logs, 1799-1974 (ADM 53)*.

Any, or all, of these logs could contain the primary record of a birth, death or marriage at sea and it would be wise to consult all of those that survive. An example of the death, and subsequent burial at sea, of Percy Hall, a merchant marine reservist serving aboard *HMS Andes* as a butcher during World War 1, is shown in Figure 18.

The log book may also record, or refer to, a death or burial of a crew member even if the event took place ashore. For instance the ship's log for *HMS Cruiser* (ADM 53/10476) records that at 3:00 p.m. on Friday 30 January 1874: 'Sent funeral party ashore to attend the burial service on the remains of the late Shedden Watson Dighton Gunner R.M.A. of this ship'.

Those record series at TNA are arranged by ship's name and date and there are good finding aids both in the reading rooms and in PROCAT, but there are no indexes to the names of men or events recorded in them. Where a ship was sunk or lost the log book is not likely to have survived, but other records could provide some useful information; details of these may be found in TNA's leaflet.[74]

It should not be overlooked that the log books of hospital ships may record deaths of patients on board. Even if the ship was of mercantile origin its log book, whilst in Admiralty service, should be found amongst the records described here. The war diaries of hospital ships, preserved at TNA in PRO series WO 95 for World War 1, do not seem however to name patients.

## Muster Books and Pay Lists

*Muster Books*
Muster books of the ship's company, which include any Royal Marines and those who were 'supernumerary for victuals only', survive at TNA in several record series, namely:

| | | |
|---|---|---|
| Ships' Musters, Series I | ADM 36 | 1688-1808 |
| Ships' Musters, Series II | ADM 37 | 1804-1842 |
| Ships' Musters, Series III | ADM 38 | 1793-1878 |
| Ships' Musters, Series IV | ADM 39 | 1667-1798 |

These series of records are arranged by ship's name and date and there are good finding aids both in the reading rooms and in PROCAT. Many muster books contain integral indexes to the names of men recorded in them. Both ratings and commissioned officers are included.

Significant about these records for our purposes is that they contain a column headed *'D, DD or R'* to signifying that a man was Discharged, Discharged Dead or Run (meaning Deserted). DD, meaning discharged dead, is normally qualified, in the column headed *'Whither or for What Reason'*, by a note of the circumstances such as 'At sea', 'Slain in battle', 'Fell from aloft'. Where no other indication is given then the death may be assumed to be from illness. A further column entitled *'Time of Discharge & Year'* would, in these circumstances, give the date of death. The term Ds means Discharged to sick quarters and could be a precursor to a death.

*Pay Lists*
In addition to the Muster Books a ship would keep a Pay Book. These too include the columns headed *'D, DD or R'*, *'Whither or for What Reason'*, and *'Time of Discharge & Year'*. These may contain more information than found in the Muster Books since men discharged dead would not be present when the ship was paid off. Both ratings and commissioned officers are included.

At least three distinct sets of pay books were compiled. That kept by the Pay Office of the Treasurer of the Navy has been preserved (ADM 33-35), until it was discontinued in 1832, as it occasionally contains entries, not found in the other sets, of payments to executors of deceased seamen. That kept by the Ticket Office or Office of the Controller of the Treasurer's Accounts (ADM 32) was preserved to continue the collection from 1832 until it too was discontinued in 1856. Both this latter set and that kept by the Office of the Controller of the Navy (ADM 31) were used to fill gaps in the main set. These records are now to be found in:

| | | |
|---|---|---|
| Ships' Pay Books: Controller's (only 8 books) | ADM 31 | 1691-1710 |
| Ships' Pay Books: Ticket Office | ADM 32 | 1692-1856 |
| Ships' Pay Books: Treasurer's, Series I | ADM 33 | 1699-1778 |
| Ships' Pay Books: Treasurer's, Series II | ADM 34 | 1766-1785 |
| Ships' Pay Books: Treasurer's, Series III | ADM 35 | 1777-1832 |

Patients in naval hospitals, hospital ships and sick quarters are mostly to be found in *Hospital Musters, 1740-1860 (ADM 102)*. Muster books for sick quarters, 1757-1758 are in ADM 30/51-52 and arrears lists, 1739-1742 in ADM 30/6. In cases where the patient did not survive one would expect a mention to be made to that effect.

**Bishop of London's Registry**

*Marriages, (1842-1889)*
From 1842 to 1879 returns, consisting of signed documents or extracts from ship's logs, related to marriages performed aboard HM ships by captains or chaplains, were sent by the captain to the Admiralty for onward transmission to the Bishop of London's Registry. In 1880 copies of these returns were forwarded by that registry to the GRO (England and Wales). From 1880 to 1889 returns were sent directly to the GRO (England and Wales). All these, covering the period 1842-1889, are now to be found in RG 33/156, wherein there is an integral index; there is also a separate index in RG 43/7. An example taken from these records is shown in Figure 19.

A record of those marriages where the return was sent to the Bishop of London's Registry is to be found at the Guildhall Library in *Bishop of London's Registry: International Memoranda (baptisms, marriages and burials) Ms 10926*. These are listed in *List of certificates of marriage on board HM ships (1843-1879)* in *Ms 11,531*; they should also be indexed in *Ms 10926C*. These records should correspond to returns described in the previous paragraph.

*Baptisms and Burials*

The Bishop of London was responsible for the examination of chaplains who were warranted by the Admiralty.[75] It is presumably for that reason that some records of baptisms and burials at sea are to be found amongst those of the Bishop of London's Registry preserved at the Guildhall Library. In addition the Bishop of Gibraltar kept a memorandum book of miscellaneous baptisms that include some performed by clergymen travelling abroad on board ship. Amongst the Guildhall Library's collections are to be found:

| Ms 10926 indexed in Ms 10926C | Bishop of London's Registry: International Memoranda (baptisms, marriages and burials) | 1816-1924 (but with some entries back to 1788) | Include some registrations made by clergymen on board ship. |
|---|---|---|---|
| Ms 23607 indexed in Ms 23607A | Bishop of Gibraltar: memorandum book of miscellaneous baptisms | 1921-1969 | |
| Ms 11817 | Certificates of baptism on British vessels | 1955–1961 | Indexed in Ms 15061/1-2 under 'Sea'. |
| Ms 11827 | Certificates of miscellaneous baptism and burial at sea | 1894–1952 | |

An example of a baptism at sea recorded in the Bishop of London's Registry is shown in Figure 20.

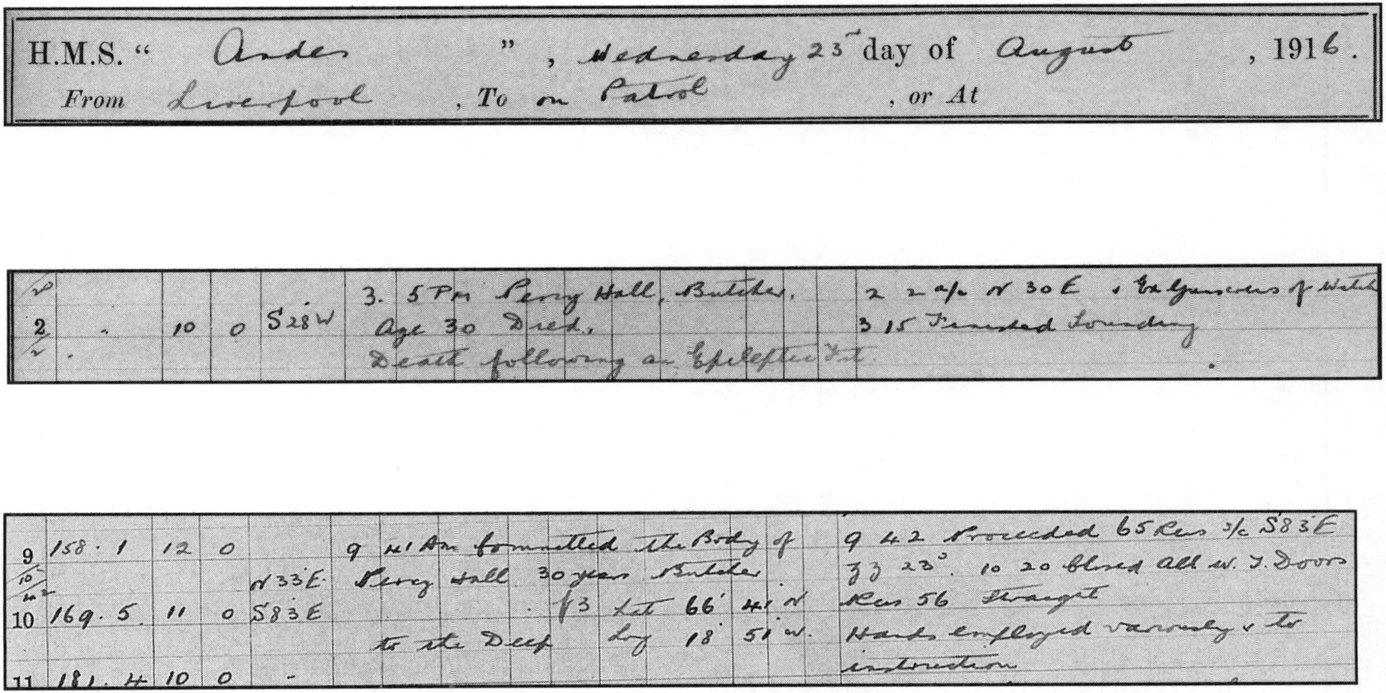
H.M.S. "Andes", Wednesday 23rd day of August, 1916.
From Liverpool, To on Patrol, or At

2 10 0 S28W 3. 5 PM Percy Hall, Butcher, Age 30 Died, Death following an Epileptic Fit.
2 2 a/c N 30 E
3 15 Finished sounding

9 158·1 12 0 9 41 Am Committed the Body of Percy Hall 30 years Butcher to the Deep
N 33 E
10 169·5 11 0 S83E Lat 66° 41' N Long 18° 51' W.
11 181·4 10 0
9 42 Proceeded 65 Revs a/c S83E
10 20 Closed all W.T. Doors
Revs 56
Hands employed variously & to instruction

*Figure 18: Death and burial at sea recorded in a Royal Navy log book:* HMS Andes, *23/25 August 1916 (PRO ADM 53/33654)*

133

20ᵗʰ November 1856

Copy of Certificate of Marriage solemnized on board Her Majestys Ship "President" by the Revᵈ J. K. Holme Chaplain. Callao the 20ᵗʰ November 1856.

76

| Names | Age | Condition | Profession | Residence |
|---|---|---|---|---|
| John Mathison | full | Batchelor | Superintendent P. S. N. C | Callao |
| Rachel Jane Dartnell | 18 | Spinster | _____ | ___ do ___ |

This marriage was solemnized between us _____  } signed { John Mathison.  Rachel Jane Dartnell.

In the presence of us

Signed {
Richᵈ Dartnell
German Loyola
Maria de Hurtado.
H. Spratt
Charles Frederick
Alex Swachan
Helena M. Dartnell.
J. S. Mould.
James Donnet.

By me  Signed  J. K. Holme

Attested copy

Charles Frederick

*Figure 19: Marriage aboard a naval ship: HMS President, 1856 (PRO RG 33/156)*

74

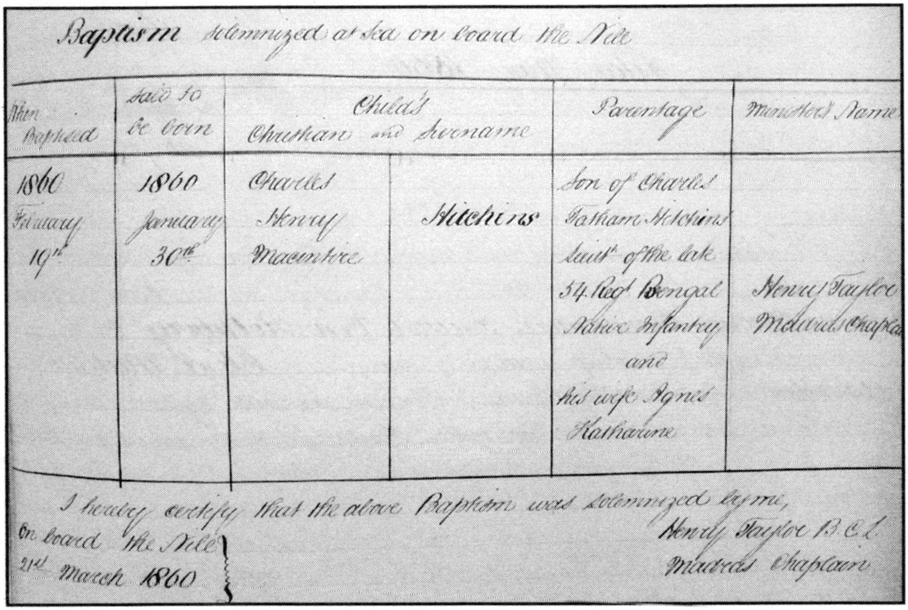

Baptism solemnized at sea on board the Nile

| When Baptized | Said to be born | Child's Christian | and Surname | Parentage | Minister's Name |
|---|---|---|---|---|---|
| 1860 February 19th | 1860 January 30th | Charles Henry Macintire | Hitchins | Son of Charles Tatham Hitchins Lieut. of the late 54 Regt. Bengal Native Infantry and his wife Agnes Katharine | Henry Taylor Madras Chaplain |

I hereby certify that the above Baptism was solemnized by me,

On board the Nile 21st March 1860

Henry Taylor B.C.L.
Madras Chaplain

*Figure 20: Baptism at sea recorded in the Bishop of London's registry:*
HMS Nile, *1860 (Guildhall Library Ms 10926/6 p. 144)*

# ADMIRALTY

## Introduction

Both the Admiralty and Navy Board maintained a number of sets of records related to births and deaths of those who served either in the Royal Navy or the Royal Marines, whether as officers, ratings or marines. These records, though they will certainly contain very many events, especially deaths, that occurred at sea, do not limit their scope to that. These secondary sources, for that is what they mostly are, are described in this chapter.

The coherence of many of the record series has not been maintained and the registers have become dispersed within their modern arrangement. Nicholas Rodger, in his book,[76] has recreated the original arrangement and this is referred to here, where appropriate by, the designation '*NAMR: Series...*' to assist with cross-referencing.

## Deaths in service (1787-1878)

### *Dead men's wages (1787-1809)*

At TNA, PRO series *Admiralty: Royal Hospital Greenwich: Miscellaneous Records (ADM 80)* includes two volumes (ADM 80/4 and 5) that comprise lists of those discharged dead where wages remained unpaid. These are arranged alphabetical but by the first letter of the surname only. In both volumes, the ships on which the man served (presumably those from which outstanding wages were due) is recorded together with his rating which is often in highly abbreviated form. Only in one of the volumes (ADM 80/5) is the date of death given. An example is shown in Figure 21.

### *Ratings (1802-1878) (NAMR: Series AF and EC)*

These volumes are a summary record of deaths of RN ratings and marines. Their purpose was to be a means of reference to the series of claims for back pay from executors and next of kin of ratings who died in service, between 1800 and 1860, now to be found in *Seaman's Effects Papers (ADM 44)*. The volumes are to be found in *Register of Seamen's Effects Papers, 1802-1861, (ADM 141)* and are continued in similar form in *Registers of Discharged Dead Cases, 1859-1878, (ADM 154)*. They are actually four sub series, namely:

|            |              |
|------------|--------------|
| 1802-1824  | ADM 141/1-3  |
| 1825-1848  | ADM 141/4-6  |
| 1849-1861  | ADM 141/7-9  |
| 1859-1878  | ADM 154/1-9  |

The volumes are either alphabetically arranged or contain a index. The alphabetical arrangement within the volumes of ADM 141 is unusual being by first letter, first vowel then next consonant irrespective of whether it comes before or after the first vowel – thus the name Smith will be found, along with Simmonds, indexed under Sim as can be seen in Figure 22. The information to be found in ADM 141 consists of: the seaman's surname and forename, any alias, the ships on which he had served (presumably for which pay was outstanding), date on which he was discharged dead (DD) and the date and method of payment; an example is shown in Figure 22. The volumes in ADM 154 are slightly less informative giving the year, seaman's surname and forename, ship, name of legal representative, documents retained (for example 'will') amount and date payment was made – no date of death is given.

*Officers and Civilians (1830-1860) (NAMR: Series ED)*
A similar series to that described above relating to claims for back pay of deceased officer is *Officers' and Civilians' Effects Papers (ADM 45).* There is a card index, available in the reading rooms at TNA, covering the first 10 of the 39 bundles.

**World War 1**

Records of those Royal Naval personnel who died during World War 1 are to be found in *Admiralty: Naval Casualties, Indexes, War Grave Rolls and Statistics Book, First World War (ADM 242).* The series is divided into two main sections as described below.

*Officers (NAMR: Series AG)*
This portion of the series (ADM 242/1-5) covers all commissioned officers, warrant officers and midshipmen killed, or who died in service from any cause, during World War 1 (1914-1920). It consists of cards on which are recorded: name, date, place and cause of death; the name and address of the next of kin are usually given on the reverse of the card. These are arranged alphabetically by the individual's name but there is a supplementary index to ships lost between 1914 and 1919 (ADM 242/6). An example of a card for an individual is shown in Figure 23.

*Ratings (NAMR: Series AH)*

This portion of the series (ADM 242/7-10) consists of an alphabetical register recording the place of burial of those who died from any cause during World War 1. Included are ratings in the Royal Navy, Royal Naval Air Service, Royal Naval Volunteer Reserve, Royal Naval Reserve and other ranks in the Royal Marines; some civilians are also included. It includes name; decorations (if any); rank or rating; official number, branch of service, ship or unit; date and place of birth; date and cause of death; place of burial; and name and address of next of kin.

A code is used to record the cause of death:

1. Killed in action or died subsequently of wounds or disease etc.

2. Killed, or subsequently died of, injuries, exposure or drowned etc.

3. Died from disease etc.

4. Suicide, murder, alcoholism, heat stroke etc.

A full description of the categories is given at the front of each volume.

Under place of burial is normally recorded the name and address of the cemetery with plot, row and grave number. Alternatively it may record 'buried at sea' or Ø indicating 'Body not recovered for burial' or × for 'No information on location of grave'.

This series is identical to that held by the General Register Office and from which they issue certificates. An example is shown in Figure 24.

**Medical Department Registers (1854 onwards)**

The registers maintained by the Medical Director-Generals' office record the deaths of individuals in the Royal Navy and the Royal Marines under four categories as described below. Some of these records are closed for 75 years.

*Killed or wounded in action (1854-1929) (NAMR: Series FA)*
This set, *Registers of Killed and Wounded, (ADM 104/140-149),* records those killed or wounded in action. It covers officers, ratings and marines.

| Dates | Registers | Indexes |
|---|---|---|
| 1854-1911 | ADM 104/144 | Internally by name |
| 1914-1915 | ADM 104/145 | Internally by name |
| 1915-1929 | ADM 104/146-149 | Internally by ship; by name in ADM 104/140-143 |

The information found there includes: name; rank or rating, ship served on; date, place and cause of death or injury. Often an individual's age is given and, for those wounded, the nature of the wound.

*Deaths other than by enemy action (1893-1956) (NAMR: Series EX)*
This set, *Registers of Reports of Death: Ships (ADM 104/102-121),* records deaths from causes other than enemy action. It covers officers, ratings, marines, coastguards, dockyard and victualling yard employees. It is arranged by ship, unit or establishment but there are nominal indexes:

| Dates | Registers | Indexes to names |
|---|---|---|
| 1893-1939 | ADM 104/109-112 | ADM 104/102-105 |
| 1940-1943 | ADM 104/113-115 | ADM 104/106 |
| 1944-1945 | ADM 104/116-117 | ADM 104/107 |
| 1946-1950 | ADM 104/118-119* | ADM 104/108 |
| 1951-1956 | ADM 104/120*-121* | internal |

These registers record: name; rank or rating; date, place and cause of death.

*Deaths by enemy action (July 1900-Oct 1941) (NAMR: Series EY)*
This set, *Registers of Reports of Deaths (ADM 104/122-126),* records deaths by enemy action. It includes marines and ratings of the naval reserves but no commissioned or warrant officers. The arrangement is alphabetical by individual's name. The information found there includes: name; rank or rating, and service number; ship served on; date, place and cause of death; date of notification of death, relative informed and sometimes the address of the next of kin.

---

\*  Closed for 75 years

*Deaths: ratings, World War 2 (1939-1948) (NAMR: Series EZ)*
This set, *Registers of Reports of Deaths: Naval Ratings (ADM 104/127-139)*, records those who died from any cause. It covers naval and reserve ratings and marines. The arrangement is alphabetical by individual's name. Recorded here are: name; official number; branch of service, rank or rating; ship or unit; date and place of birth; date, cause and place of death; decorations (if any).

The place of death often records simply 'at sea'. The cause of death is in general terms and uses a numerical code:

1. Died on war service
2. Missing – death on war service

3. Died from natural causes
4. Suicide
5. Death from other causes

*Deaths: officers, World War 2*
There are no special registers, at TNA, related to the deaths of officers during World War 2. Information about them should be sought from:

- Deaths other than by enemy action (1893-1956) described above

- Commonwealth War Graves Commission – Debt of Honour, available on the internet at www.cwgc.org

- Naval Officers' War Deaths, 1939-1948, at the General Register Office for England and Wales, described in the chapter Registrars-General of Births, Deaths and Marriages

## Royal Marines

Each Division of the Royal Marines maintained its own registers of births, deaths and marriages. Some events recorded in them may have taken place at sea. The surviving registers are now to be found in:

| | | |
|---|---|---|
| Chatham Division | 1830-1913 | ADM 183/114-120 |
| Plymouth Division | 1862-1920 | ADM 184/43-54 |
| Woolwich Division (marriage registers only) | 1822-1869 | ADM 81/23-25 |
| Royal Marine Artillery | 1810-1853 | ADM 193/9 |
| | 1866-1921 | ADM 5/437 |
| Portsmouth Division (marriage registers only) | 1869-1881 | ADM 185/69 |

## Naval Chaplains

*Registers of baptism, confirmations, marriages and burials (ADM 338)* contains records of these services performed by naval chaplains. The covering dates are 1845 to 1995 but most refer to the second half of the 20th century and to shore establishments in the UK.

## Miscellaneous

*Mediterranean Station: Correspondence and Papers, 1843-1968 (ADM 121)* includes records of the deaths and burials of RN personnel, both officers and ratings, in addition to records of births and baptisms of their children. Similar material may be found in the miscellaneous series of *Admiralty: Service Records, Registers, Returns and Certificates, 1673-1960 (ADM 6)*; in particular burials for Ireland Island, Bermuda (1826-1946) are in ADM 6/434 and 436. Also found there are baptisms for Ireland Island, Bermuda (1826-1946) in ADM 6/434 and 435 and for Boaz Garrison, Bermuda (1903-1918) in ADM 6/439.

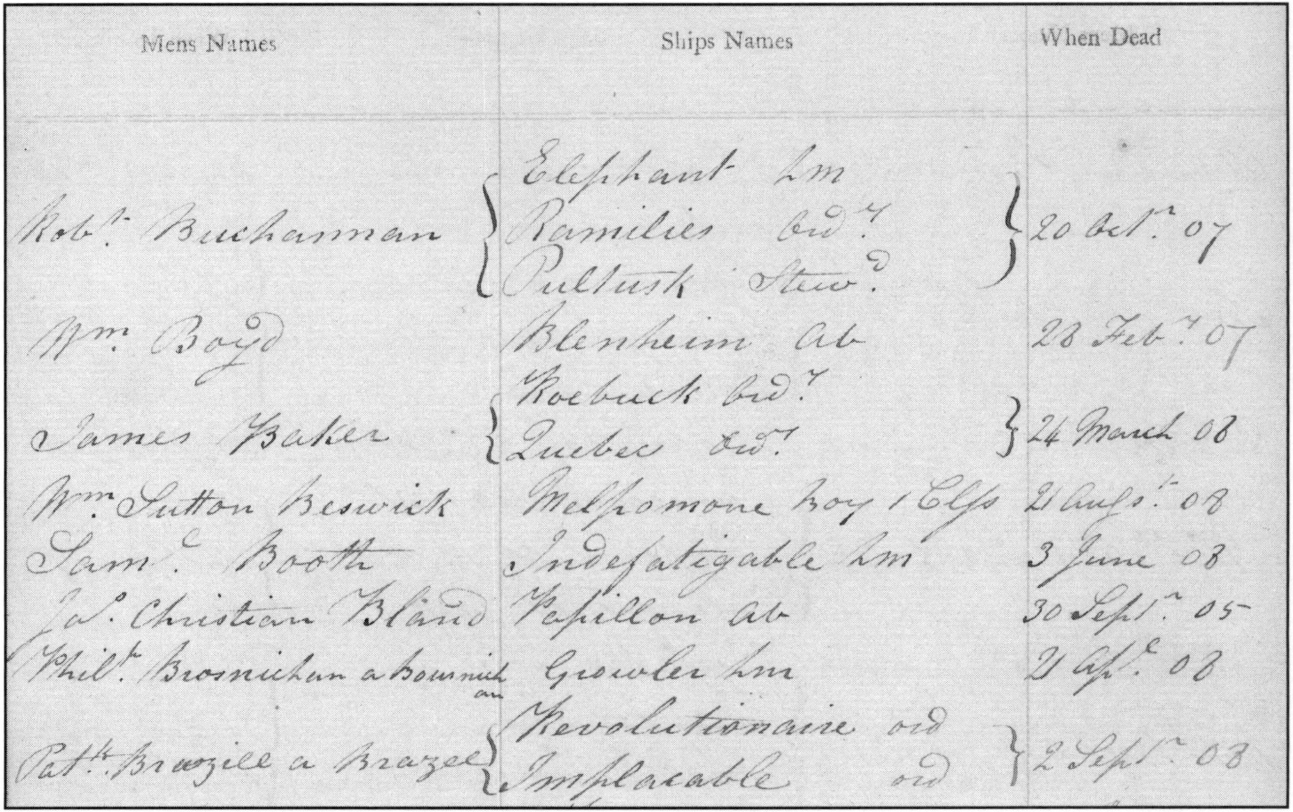

| Mens Names | Ships Names | When Dead |
| --- | --- | --- |
| Robt. Buchannan | Elephant Lm<br>Ramilies ditto<br>Pultusk Stewd. | 20 Octr. 07 |
| Wm. Boyd | Blenheim Ab | 28 Feby. 07 |
| James Baker | Roebuck ditto<br>Quebec ditto | 24 March 08 |
| Wm. Sutton Beswick | Melpomone boy 1 Cls | 21 Augst. 08 |
| Saml. Booth | Indefatigable Lm | 3 June 08 |
| Jas. Christian Bland | Papillon Ab | 30 Septr. 05 |
| Philt. Brosnihan a Bournich | Growler Lm | 21 Apl. 08 |
| Patk. Breazile a Brazeal | Revolutionaire ord<br>Implacable ord | 2 Septr. 08 |

Figure 21: Register of dead men's wages, Royal Navy (PRO ADM 80/5)

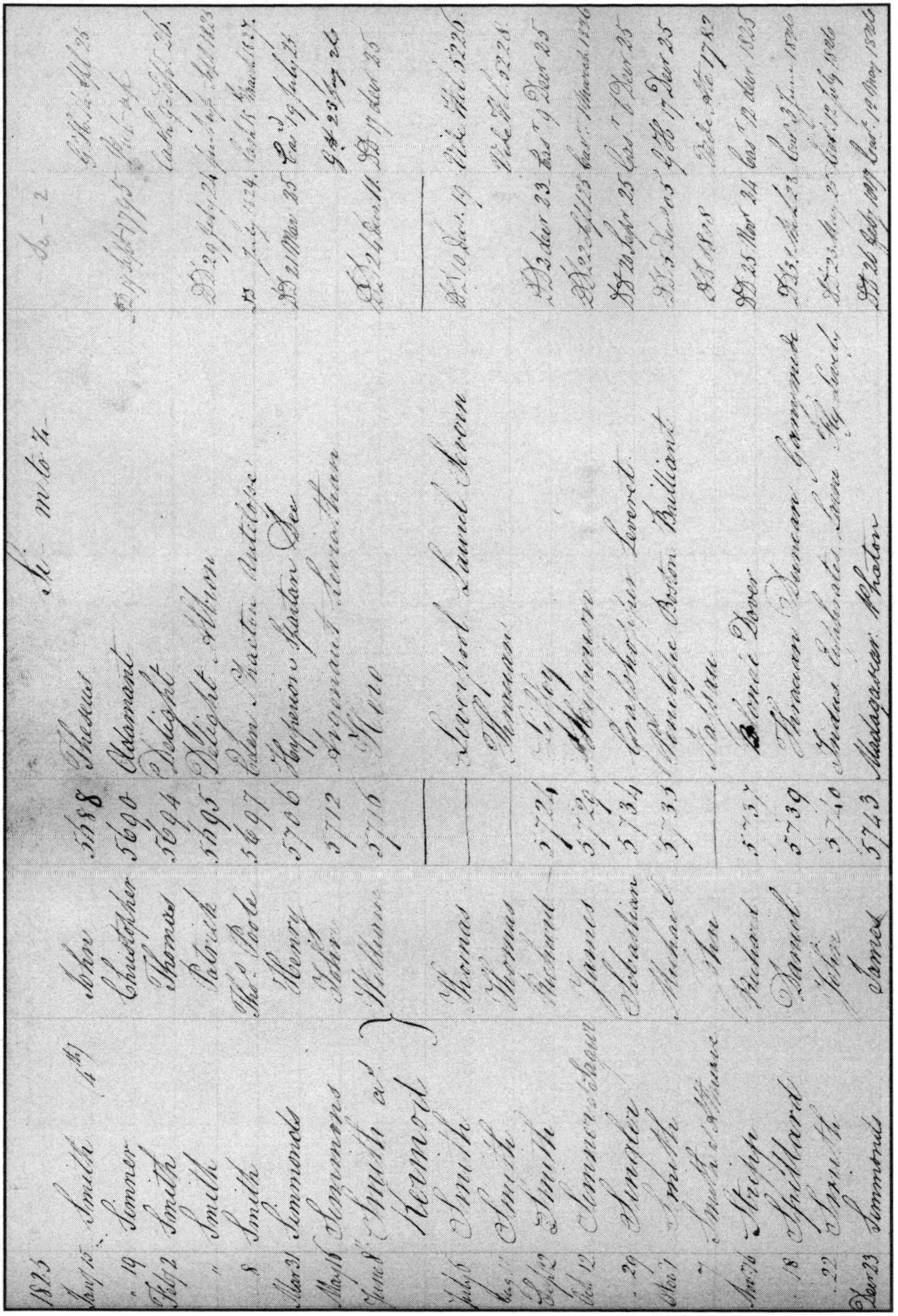

Figure 22: Register of Seamen's Effects Papers, 1825 (PRO ADM 141/6)

CASUALTIES—NAVAL OFFICERS.

Docket No. *1973*

Surname and initials ... HEARN, HENRY J.

Rank ....... Lieut Commdr.

Branch of Service ... R.N. (S/m "K17")

Place of death ... at Sea, *off mouth of Firth of Forth*

Place of burial ...

Date of death ... 31ˢᵗ January 1918

Cause........ Drowned on active Service

Sunk in collision N. Coast of Scotland

[2623 G 195 10m 11/1- T1673 G & S 110

Mother

Mrs Hearn
Bycroft
Church Stretton
Shropshire

*Figure 23: RN Officers deaths, World War 1 (PRO ADM 242/3)*

| NAME (Surname first) | Decorations (if any) | Rating | Official No. and Port Division | Branch of Service | Ship or Unit | Date and place of birth | Date of Death | Cause of Death | Name and Address of Cemetery | Location of Grave | | | Relatives notified and their address | Remarks |
|---|---|---|---|---|---|---|---|---|---|---|---|---|---|---|
| | | | | | | | | | | Plot | Row | Grave No. | | |
| STEPHEN. William Caesar, | - | E.R.A. | 1810 E.A. (Dev.) | R.N.R. | H.M. "Teafler" "Cuper". | 24.1.84. Liverpool. | 17.5.19. | 1. | Peel Cem. Peel, Isle of Man. | New | - | 664 | Widow, Irene M, Mona Cottage, Glen Wllyn, Kirk Michael, Isle of Man. | |
| STEPHENS. Albert Edmund, | * | Lce. Cpl. | Po/17563 | R.M.L.I. 1st R.M. Bat-n.R.N.D. | 13.2.96. Kingsbury, Warwick. | 28.4.17. | 1. | Orchard Dump Cemetery, Arleux-en-Gohelle,France. | 6 | G | 3 | Sister, Mrs. Edge, 34 Station St, Bloxwich, Nr. Walsall; Staffs. | |
| STEPHENS. Albert Edward, | | Ch. Sh. Ck. (Pensr.) | 159760 (Dev.) | R.N. | H.M.S. "Vi-id". | 20.1.72. Fourshells, Hants. | 19.4.15. | 3 | Plymouth,Devonport & Stone-house Cemetery,(Church Gound) Plymouth.Devon. | S. | 2. | 8. | Father, James, Oak Road, Purlie, Hythe, Southampton. | |
| STEPHENS. Albert Edward Victor, | * | Boy I. | J.27232 (PO) | R.N. | H.M.S. "Viktor". | 14.7.98. Bristol, Glos. | 13.1.15. | 2. | ∅ | | | | Sister, Grace Morgan, 1 Marsh Lane, Barton Hill, Bristol. | |
| STEPHENS. Alfred William, | * | Ch. E.A. 2nd. | 347457 (Dev.) | R.N. | H.M.S. "Lion". | 16.1.85. Brixham, Devon. | 31.5.16. | 1. | Buried at sea. | | | | Widow, Ethel M, Gaudon, 116 Windsor Rd, Ellscombe,Torquay. | |
| STEPHENS. Arthur Kingdon, | * | Asst. Construct-or. 2nd. (Admiralty) | Nil (Dev.) | Civ-lian. | H.M.S. "Queen Mary". | 5.9.90. Plymouth. | 31.5.16. | 1. | ∅ | | | | Father, William, Caseytown, Whitchurch, Tavistock,S.Devon. | |
| STEPHENS. Charles, | - | Sig. Boy | 236 S.B. (Dev.) | R.N.R. | H.M.Yacht "Venesla". | 29.12.99. Southell, Lisbeard, Cornwall. | 24.8.17. | 2 | Falmouth Cemetery, Falmouth,Cornwall. | K. | H. | 49. | Father, Fred, Vine Cottage, Ringmore, Teignmouth,Devon. | |
| STEPHENS. Charles Wesley, | * | W.T. Op. 1st. | 117 W.T.S. (Dev.) | R.N.R. | H.M.Tug "Char". | 27.4.82. Manchester. | 16.1.15. | 2. | ∅ | | | | Father, Robert Stevens, 297 St.Clowes Street, Higher Broughton, Manchester. | |
| STEPHENS. David Albert, | * | A.B. | Wales Z/985 (Dev.) | R.N.V.R. | H.M.S. "Invisible". | 16.6.80. N.K. | 31.5.16. | 1. | ∅ | | | | Widow, Catherine, 1 Amberton Place, Pengydarren, Merthyr, Wales. | |

*Figure 24: RN Ratings deaths, World War 1 (PRO ADM 242/10)*

Folio No. 000143

| | 1 NAME (Surname first) | 2 FORM DIVISION and OFFICIAL NO. | 3 BRANCH OF SERVICE. | 4 RATING | 5 SHIP OR UNIT. | 6 DATE OF BIRTH. | 7 PLACE OF BIRTH. | 8 DATE OF DEATH. | 9 CAUSE OF DEATH. | 10 PLACE OF DEATH. | 11 DECORATIONS (if any) |
|---|---|---|---|---|---|---|---|---|---|---|---|
| 1. | BREEN, Patrick | LY/KX.99613 | R.N.F.S. | Sto.1. | H.M.S. TORRENT | 1.1.1919 | Stevenston, Ayrshire | 3.4.1941 | 3. | At Sea | |
| 2. | BREEN, Thomas | LY/KX.101273 | R.N.F.S. | Sto. | H.M.T. PINGER | 20.12.1896 | Wexford, Eire | 12.8.1940 | 2. | At Sea | |
| 3. | BREEN, William | P/DD/X.28338 | R.N.V.R. | A.B. | H.M.S. UNIQUE | 8.5.1918 | Springburn, Glasgow | 23.10.1942 | 2. | At Sea | |
| 4. | BREENS, Roy Douglas | P/CX.521354 | R.N. | Ord.Sea. | H.M.S. CAIRO | 7.1.1923 | Barking, Essex. | 3.7.1944 | 3. | At Sea | |
| 5. | BREETSELAAR, Arie | 412316 | - | Dutch Airman Gunner | M.V. PRINS WILLEM III | Not Known | Not Known | 29.3.1943 | 1. | On board H.M.S. LADY HOGARTH | |
| 6. | BREEZE, Albert John | P/CX.270123 | R.N. | A.B. | H.M.S. TRINIDAD | 4.8.1915 | Bethnal Green, London | 14.5.1942 | 2. | At Sea | |
| 7. | BREEZE, Charles Allen | P/KX.85187 | R.N. | Cook (S) | H.M.S. QUEEN ELIZABETH | 5.9.1922 | Attleborough, Norfolk | 20.6.1943 | 5. Accidental drowning | Hampton Roads, Virginia, U.S.A. | |
| 8. | BREEZE, Ernest Frederick Seccombe | C/JX.21308 | R.N. | A/P.O. (Ty) | H.M.S. PRESIDENT III (S.S. SHENLEY) | 13.10.1913 | Dovercourt, Essex. | 17.4.1943 | 3. | At Sea | |
| 9. | BREEZE, James | P/CX.130135 | R.N. | Sto.1. | H.M.S. STEVENSTONE | 21.3.1911 | Parkdale, Glam. | 30.11.1944 | 2. | At Sea | |
| 10. | BREEZE, Stanley | D/MX.636540 | R.N. | S.B.A. Probl. | H.M.S. GOULD | 5.1.1903 | Standish, Lancs. | 1.3.1944 | 2. | At Sea | |
| 11. | BREHAUT, John Edward | O/SSX.29329 | R.N. | s/Lt. P.O.(Ty) | H.M.S. AFRIDUR | 13.12.1920 | Loughborough, Leics. | 16.11.1942 | 2. | At Sea | |
| 12. | BREMER, Reginald Herbert Ronald | CH/X.103637 | R.N. | Sgt.(Ty) | 47 R.M. Commando | 2.6.1922 | Bermondsey, London | 2.11.1944 | 4. | Holland | |

*Figure 25: RN Ratings deaths, World War 2 (PRO ADM 104/128)*

# REGISTRARS-GENERAL OF BIRTHS, DEATHS AND MARRIAGES

## Introduction

In the chapter on Legislation and Regulations we discovered just what records should have been created. Now we will look at what has actually survived and over what period, what it contains, where it is to be found, and how it is arranged.

This specific chapter is concerned with the registers created by the several Registrars-General of Births, Deaths and Marriages (GROs) related to events that occurred aboard both Royal Navy and merchant ships. The information on which these registers are based could have come directly from the commanding officers of such vessels or have been forwarded, with or without filtering, by the RGSS, the Admiralty or other officials. As such it must be recognised that the GROs' registers are not primary sources and that they are at least two if not three stages removed from the original record. This means that it is inevitable that they will contain errors and omissions for that reason alone. In addition it is known that they are incomplete as a consequence of the selection processes applied during the transmission of the data to the GROs. So if a search in these records fails to reveal an appropriate entry then there is still more research to be done – this aspect is addressed more fully in the next chapter.

Here we shall be discussing the records compiled by the various GROs, but not all of them are still with those GROs. For instance some miscellaneous records from the GRO for England and Wales are now at TNA, mostly in the RG series. Some duplicate consular registers are also to found there in the various FO series. Additionally TNA hold a few similar records, notably in the CO series, that did not actually originate with any GRO but, for convenience, all this material is considered in this chapter.

## England and Wales

Certain material mentioned in the chapter on Legislation and Regulations is known not to survive, and we may therefore dismiss any further consideration of it; namely:

- The certified copy of the minute, or log book entry, sent by the master of a British vessel to the General Register Office for England and Wales does not survive. The original minute may possibly survive, the log book should survive, the GRO's entry in the Marine Register survives but the certified copy referred to in the legislation does not.

- Details of births and deaths, extracted from inward passenger lists, sent by emigration or customs officials to the General Register Office do not survive. The original passenger list may possibly survive, the log book should survive, the GRO's entry in the Marine Register survives but the copy referred to in the legislation does not survive.

- Details of births and deaths, extracted from outward passenger lists (Master's List), deposited on arrival, and landing of the passengers, in a foreign port either with HM's Consul or with the Chief Officer of Customs if the port was in a British possession do not survive. Whether an entry was made, based on this information, in the GRO's Marine Register, is unclear but the copy referred to in the legislation does not.

*Marine Registers*
Marine Register of Births (1837-1965)
The categories of events included in this key series of records are:

| From | Categories included: | Applicability |
|---|---|---|
| 1 July 1837 to 1874 | Births taking place on a British vessel where the parent was an English or Welsh subject. | • Royal Navy ships<br>• British merchant ships<br>These consist of certified copies of minutes, or copies of log book entries, sent by the captains of British merchant and Royal Navy ships directly to the GRO. |
| 1855 | Births taking place on board ships carrying passengers to/from UK | • Ships carrying passengers to/from, the UK from/to places outside Europe and not within the Mediterranean<br>  • includes those joining the vessel within Europe etc.<br>  • does not apply to territories under the jurisdiction of the East India Company[*] |

---

[*] The Passenger Act 1855, 18 & 19 Vic c.119 s.99 provided for the Governor General of India in Council to adopt these provisions. No check has been made to see if this was ever done.

| From | Categories included: | Applicability |
|------|---------------------|---------------|
| 1875 | Births taking place on board where the father or, if the child was a bastard, the mother, was not a Scottish or Irish subject. | • Royal Navy ships<br>• British merchant ships<br>• All non-British ships, with ports of departure or destination within the UK, carrying passengers<br><br>These consist of returns made by the RGSS, for merchant vessels, and by the captains of Royal Navy vessels. |
| 1922 | Births taking place on board Irish-registered merchant ships | • these appear to have only been received for the one year, namely 1924<br><br>*Note:* Reference to these is made in the Abstract of Arrangements[77] but no separate register has been located and it is presumed that details are recorded in the Marine Register of Births. |

*Notes:* These regulations applied to all places where the laws of the United Kingdom applied. But, from 1894, they did not apply to dominion or colonial ships within the jurisdiction of the Government of the British possession to which they belonged.

Births on board vessels in territorial waters should be registered with the local Registrar of Births and so ought to be recorded in the general series of birth registers but may not always have been.

Indexes to these registers are available at the Family Records Centre or, on microfiche, at many locations world-wide including the library of the Society of Genealogists. They give the name of the child and, from 1876 onwards, the name of the ship (but the prefix HMS does not seem to be used for RN vessels).

In addition to the above there is a small set of *Informal Certificates of Births at Sea* comprising some 41 entries covering the years 1839-1856. There is a separate index to these, although an entry bearing the words 'See Informal Certificates' may be found in the index to marine births proper. These records relate to births where the event could not be correctly registered.

This could be for a number of reasons such as: the birth was reported directly to a local registrar who then forwarded details to the GRO; the GRO was notified of the birth by an interested party, such as a parent; or where the correct form of words certifying a report had not been used by the master.

From 1966 onwards entries that would have been recorded here will now be found in the *Registers of Births Abroad*. There are composite indexes to these giving the child's name but noting the post as 'Shipping' without recording the name of the vessel.

Information from any of these registers can be obtained, in the form of certified copies, by personal, postal, telephone or e-mail application to the GRO. The level of information given in these entries varies considerably; sometimes they will record the position in latitude and longitude (lat/long), as in the example below.

---

Liverpool
Feby 25th 1854

Sir

I beg leave to furnish you with a copy of the minute which has been made in the log book of the Barque Jane Morice respecting the birth of my son William Guy Browne.

Novr. 9th 1853 at 2 a.m. Mrs Browne was delivered of a male child in lat 15° 40' N and long 29° 19' W.
The childs name is William Guy Browne
The Fathers Joseph Browne
The Mothers maiden name Ann Floyd Evett Chapman
Fathers profession – Master Mariner
Signature Joseph Browne
Residence No. 8 Chester Street, Foxteth Park, Liverpool

I hereby certify that this is a true copy of the minute made in the log book of the Barque Jane Morice of Liverpool on the 9th day of Novr. 1853
Witness my hand this 25th day of Feby. 1854

(Signed) Joseph Browne
Captain of Barque Jane Morice

A true copy     George Graham
                Registrar General

---

The *Index to Marine Registers of Birth, 1837-1862* records Browne, William Guy p.194 and the corresponding certificate reads as above. A copy of an early entry in the *Marine Register of Births* is shown in Figure 26.

Marine Register of Deaths (1837-1965)
The *Marine Register of Deaths* is the key series of records relating to deaths at sea. The categories of events included are:

| From | Categories included: | Applicability |
|---|---|---|
| 1 July 1837 to 1874 | Deaths of English or Welsh subjects taking place on a British vessel | • Royal Navy ships<br><br>• British merchant ships<br>*Note:* These requirements may have been widely interpreted not to cover crew – *see* note below.<br><br>These consist of certified copies of minutes, or copies of log book entries, sent by the captains of British merchant and Royal Navy ships directly to the GRO. |
| 1855 | Deaths taking place on board ships carrying passengers to/from UK | • Ships carrying passengers to/from, the UK from/to places outside Europe and not within the Mediterranean<br><br>*Notes:*<br>  • includes those joining the vessel within Europe etc.<br>  • does not apply to territories under the jurisdiction of the East India Company (*see* footnote on page 88) |
| 1875 | Deaths taking place on board where the deceased was not a Scottish or Irish subject | • Royal Navy ships<br><br>• British merchant ships<br><br>• All non-British ships, with ports of departure or destination within the UK, carrying passengers<br><br>These consist of returns made by the RGSS, for merchant vessels, and by the captains of Royal Navy vessels (*see* note below related to the war periods). |

| From | Categories included: | Applicability |
|------|---------------------|---------------|
| 1922 | Deaths taking place on board Irish-registered merchant ships | • these appear to have only been received for the one year, namely 1924.<br><br>_Note:_ Reference to these is made in the Abstract of Arrangements[78] but no separate register has been located and it is presumed that details are recorded in the Marine Register of Deaths. |

_Notes:_ These regulations applied to all places where the laws of the United Kingdom applied. But, from 1894, they did not apply to dominion or colonial ships within the jurisdiction of the Government of the British possession to which they belonged.

Deaths on board vessels in territorial waters should be registered with the local Registrar of Deaths and so ought to be recorded in the general series of death registers but may not always have been.

Whilst details of all deaths recorded on crew lists, prior to 1874, should have been reported directly to the GRO it would be unwise to rely on this. A check made in the Marine Deaths Index, for England and Wales, for the 12 seamen discharged as dead from Cornish ships in 1851, all of whom gave places of birth in England, failed to reveal any of them. It may be that the legislation requiring reporting of deaths was thought not to apply to crew.

After 1894, particulars of deaths of merchant seamen who had been discharged sick, or who from other causes had recently left British vessels, would often have been recorded in the log book and in the registers of the RGSS. These entries would not have been reported to the GRO and so will not be found in these registers.

During the war periods (1914-1921 and 3 September 1939 to 30 June 1948) some returns of death continued to be sent to the GRO by the commanding officers of HM ships but such deaths are mostly recorded in the Service Registers described later. The reporting directly from HM ships resumed generally on 1 July 1948.

Indexes to these registers are available at the Family Records Centre or, on microfiche, at many locations world-wide including the library of the Society of Genealogists. They give the name of the deceased and, from 1876 onwards, the deceased's age and the name of the ship (but the prefix HMS does not seem to be used for RN vessels).

In addition to the above there are two small volumes of informal returns, namely:

- *Miscellaneous Returns: Informal Certificates of Deaths at Sea* comprising some 105 entries covering the years 1838-1868. These records relate to births, on merchant ships, where the event could not be correctly registered. This could be for a number of reasons such as: the death was reported directly to a local registrar who then forwarded details to the GRO; the GRO was notified of the birth by an interested party; or where the correct form of words certifying a report had not been used by the master. There is no separate index to this volume although an entry bearing the words 'See Informal Certificates' may be found in the index to marine deaths proper. A copy of the internal index to this volume is available at the Family Records Centre.

- *Miscellaneous Naval Deaths* covering the years, approximately, 1843-1926. It contains notifications and correspondence related to deaths aboard Royal Navy vessels. There is no separate index to this volume although an entry bearing the words 'See Admiralty Returns' may be found in the index to marine deaths proper. A copy of the internal index to this volume is available at the Family Records Centre.

From 1966 onwards entries that would have been recorded here will now be found in the *Registers of Deaths Abroad*. There are composite indexes to these giving the deceased's name but noting the post as 'Shipping' without recording the name of the vessel.

Information from any of these registers can be obtained, in the form of certified copies, by personal, postal, telephone or e-mail application to the GRO.

A typical entry in the *Index to Marine Registers of Death* reads:

| Year | Name | Age | Vessel | Page |
|------|------|-----|--------|------|
| 1894 | Cater, A.B. | 23 | J.M. Lennard | 457 |

The corresponding certificate reads:

| Return of Death of Seaman reported to the Registrar-General of Shipping and Seamen under the provisions of the 'Merchant Shipping Act 1854,' and 'Births and Deaths Registration Act, 1874,' and otherwise, during the month of October, 1894. | | | | | |
|---|---|---|---|---|---|
| Registrar-General to whom Death is required by the Act of 1874 to be reported | Name and Surname of Deceased | | Sex | Age | Rank, Profession or Occupation |
| E | CATER, A.B. | | Male | 23 | Asst. Engineer |
| Nationality or Birthplace | Last Place or Abode | | Death | | |
| | | | Cause | Date | Place |
| London | (London) | | Drowned; vessel grounded capsized and sank | 20.8.1894 | Goole Reach, R. Ouse |
| Name of ship | Official Number | Port of Registry | Trade | Source of Information | Reference to Register |
| (S.S.) J.M. Lennard | 70,435 | Middlesbro' | Foreign | C & 3 | 1B.Z./b |

It will be noted that although this death took place in territorial waters it is in fact recorded in the *Marine Deaths Register*. The level of information given in these entries varies considerably with time; those related to deaths that genuinely took place at sea will often record the position in lat/long.

It is unclear as to whether deaths of service personnel at sea would, from 1881 onwards, be recorded in the *Marine Deaths Register* or in one of the various service or, if appropriate, war death registers, so it would be wise to check both; details are given below.

*Overseas registers*
Births and Deaths
Although births and deaths at sea should be recorded in the appropriate marine register, this did not always happen. The event was sometimes reported to the consul at the next port and will be found recorded in their registers. It is therefore worth consulting these, for foreign countries where there was a British embassy or consulate:

- *Consular Registers of Birth, 1849-1965*

- *Consular Registers of Death, 1849-1965*

or, for Commonwealth countries following their independence:

- *UK High Commission Registers of Birth, 1950-1965*
- *UK High Commission Registers of Death, 1940-1981*

Both of these are continued, from 1966 in the *Registers of Births Abroad* and the *Registers of Deaths Abroad.*

Indexes to these registers are available at the Family Records Centre or, on microfiche, at many locations world-wide. Information from any of these registers can be obtained, in the form of certified copies, by personal, postal, telephone or e-mail application to the GRO.

Duplicates of some of the consular registers are available at TNA in various FO series. Lists of available registers, arranged by country are to be found in two printed works.[79] An example of such a birth, taking place near the Cape Verde Islands but registered at Shanghai, is shown in Figure 27. Many more deaths than births are recorded in these registers, for example:

| Deaths within the District of the British Consulate at *Archangel in the Empire of Russia* | | | |
|---|---|---|---|
| **When and where died** | **Name and Surname** | **Sex** | **Age** |
| *7 June 1865 NS at sea on voyage to Archangel* | *Thomas Savory Gilpin* | *male* | *34* |
| **Rank or Profession** | **Residence at the time of Death** | **Signature, Description and Residence of Informant** | **When Registered** |
| *Shipmaster Nr. of Cer. 4954* | *'Minnie' of Ipswich Nr 52703* | *Hlrum Parish Mate of the 'Minnie'* | *28 June 10 July 1865* |

**Register of Deaths, Archangel, 1849-1915 (PRO FO 267/46)**

*Note:* NS = New Style. The New Style, Gregorian, calendar was not adopted in Russia until the 20th century. At this date there was a difference of 12 days between the calendars used in Russia and in the UK.[80]

Certain miscellaneous registers may also contain references to births, marriages and deaths of British and Commonwealth subjects aboard British or foreign ships. The General Register Office (England and Wales) formerly held these, but they are now preserved at TNA:

RG 32  Miscellaneous Foreign Returns                          1831 - 1951
RG 33  Foreign Registers and Returns                          1627 - 1958
RG 35  Foreign Deaths                                         1830 - 1921
RG 36  Registers and Returns of Birth, Marriage and Death     1895 - 1950
       in the Protectorates etc of Africa and Asia
RG 43  Miscellaneous Foreign Returns of Birth, Marriage       1627 - 1947
       and Death: Indexes

The following are specifically known to contain a record of some events at sea:

| Reference | Indexed in | |
|---|---|---|
| RG 32/1-16 | RG 43/2 | Some births and baptisms at sea, 1831-1931 |
| RG 35/16 (in French) | RG 43/3 | Deaths of British citizens aboard French ships, 1836-1871 |
| RG 35/17 (in Dutch) | RG 43/3 | Deaths of British citizens aboard Dutch ships, 1839-1871 |
| CO 386 /170-172 | | Registers of deaths of emigrants at sea, 1847-1869 [CO 386/170 also records births but usually only as numbers without giving any names] |

Some notifications of deaths of prisoners of war for the World War 2 period are included in the series *General Register Office: Miscellaneous Foreign Returns (RG 32)*.

The personal information in the *Registers of deaths of emigrants at sea, 1847-1869*, is often very limited. The entry for the *Whitby*[81] which departed from London on 15 February 1849 destined for the colony of Port Phillip arriving there on 28 June recorded that it was carrying 30 married and 37 single males, 30 married and 19 single females, together with 17 boys and 25 girls aged between 1 and 14 years plus 3 boys and 1 girl under the age of 1 year. But it simply notes the death of Martha Louisa Carter, aged 38 and George Draper aged 24 plus 5 births with no additional details at all. A certificate presumably given to widower and preserved in private papers records much more:

> *Barque Whitby of London*
> *21st day of March 1849*

> *This is to certify that I Francis Sherlock by appointment of the Colonial Land and Emigration Commissioners Religious Teacher and School-master on board the above vessel (there being no clergyman on board,) on Friday the sixteenth day of March 1849, at the hour of 10 o'clock of the forenoon, Nautical Time, and at Latitude 13° 14' 45" North Longitude 22° 54' 50" West did read the Service for the Burial of the Dead for those who died at Sea, according to the Rites and Ceremonies of the United Church of England and Ireland, when the body of Martha Louisa Carter deceased wife of John Benjamin Carter Emigrant to Port Phillip was committed to the deep.*

The certificate is signed by Francis Sherlock and by the Surgeon Superintendent and the Captain.

## Marriages

The commanding officer of a Royal Naval vessel could, under certain circumstances, perform the marriage ceremony. Details of these events, from 1842 to 1889, were once available at the GRO but have now been transferred to TNA. They are to be found there in RG 33/156. They have both an integral index and are indexed in RG 43/7. They are described here in the Royal Navy chapter under Bishop of London's Registry.

The Marriage Act 1890 made legal the performance of a marriage on board an HM vessel on foreign station, where one or both parties was British, by the captain as if he were a consul. One would expect to find any such marriages to be recorded in the *Consular Registers of Marriage, 1849-1965* and subsequently in the *Register of Marriages Abroad*. Indexes to these registers are available at the Family Records Centre or, on microfiche, at many locations world-wide. Information from any of these registers can be obtained, in the form of certified copies, by personal, postal, telephone or e-mail application to the GRO. It is possible that *Foreign Marriages, 1826-1921 (RG 34)* may contain some entries related to marriages at sea.

*Service Registers*

It is unclear as to whether deaths of service personnel at sea, from 1881 onwards, would be recorded in the *Marine Deaths Register* or in one of the various service, or if appropriate war death, registers so it would be wise to check both. The death of Lord Kitchener, which took place when *HMS Hampshire* was sunk off the Orkneys in May 1916, is recorded in the *Army Officers War Deaths (1914-1921) Register*[82] and not in the *Marine Deaths Register*.

There are several series of registers that apply to service personnel abroad and during war periods, namely:

| Period | Title | Comment |
|---|---|---|
| 1761-1924 | Regimental Registers of Birth | • births of children of serving soldiers in the UK and abroad (from *c.*1790) |
| 1796-1880 | Army Chaplains' Returns of Births, Marriages and Deaths | • these relate to events abroad |
| 1881-1955 | Army [and other services] Returns of Births, Marriages and Deaths | • these relate to events abroad<br>• despite their name they do contain entries related to the other services<br>• there are separate indexes for each event giving name, station and year |
| 1956-1965 | Service Department Registers of Births, Marriages and Deaths | • these relate to events abroad<br>• there are separate indexes for each event giving name, station and year |
| 1899-1902 | War Deaths: Natal and South Africa Forces | |
| 1914-1921 | Army, Other Ranks, War Deaths | |

| Period | Title | Comment |
|--------|-------|---------|
| 1914-1921 | Army, Officers, War Deaths | |
| 1914-1921 | Naval War Deaths* | |
| 1914-1921 | Indian Services War Deaths | |
| 1939-1948 | Army, Other Ranks, War Deaths | |
| 1939-1948 | Army, Officers, War Deaths | |
| 1939-1948 | Naval Ratings, War Deaths* | |
| 1939-1948 | Naval Officers, War Deaths | |
| 1939-1948 | RAF War Deaths | |
| 1939-1948 | Indian Services War Deaths | |

Indexes to these registers are available at the Family Records Centre or, on microfiche, at many locations world-wide. Information from any of these registers can be obtained, in the form of certified copies, by personal, postal, telephone or e-mail application to the GRO.

## Scotland

*GRO: Edinburgh*

Marine Registers (1855-1974)

The *Marine Register of Births, 1855- 1971 (GROS: MIN 1-9)* is the key historic series of records relating to births at sea of children to a Scottish parent. From 1975 onwards events are recorded in *the Consular and Foreign Records New Series: Combined Series (GROS: MIN 278 -)* The Marine Register of Births is subdivided into sections, namely:

---

\*     Certificates issued by the GRO from these registers may summarise the cause of death given therein so it is wise to check the copy of the register held at TNA – *see* pages 77-78 and 80.

| Date | Reference | Title | Description |
|------|-----------|-------|-------------|
| 1855-1874 | GROS: MIN 1 | Births: Intimations | Minutes, or copies of log book entries, sent by the captains of British merchant and Royal Navy ships directly to the GRO. These should have been entered in the registers (GROS: MIN 3-5) |
| 1854-1891 | GROS: MIN 2 | Births: not registered | Probably informal notifications concerning births at sea received from individuals. |
| 1855-1876 | GROS: MIN 3-5 | Births: Register | Register of births at sea compiled from:<br>• Intimations (GROS: MIN 1)<br>• Reports of births aboard ships of any nationality carrying passengers to/from, the UK from/to places outside Europe and not within the Mediterranean<br>*Notes:*<br>• includes those joining the vessel within Europe etc.<br>• does not apply to territories under the jurisdiction of the East India Company* |
| 1875-1971 | GROS: MIN 6-9 | Returns | Returns of births received from the RGSS; these should include events on:<br>• British merchant ships<br>• All non-British ships, with ports of departure or destination within the UK, carrying passengers |

---

* The Passenger Act 1855, 18 & 19 Vic c.119 s.99 provided for the Governor General of India in Council to adopt these provisions. No check has been made to see if this was ever done.

*Notes:* These regulations applied to all places where the laws of the United Kingdom applied. But, from 1894, they did not apply to dominion or colonial ships within the jurisdiction of the Government of the British possession to which they belonged.

Births on board vessels in territorial waters should be registered with the local Registrar of Births and so ought to be recorded in the general series of birth registers but may not always have been.

From 1894 ships employed exclusively in trading between ports on the coasts of Scotland were exempt from the requirement to keep log books. It seems likely that any births were reported to a local registrar and thence to the GRO and RGSS. As most voyages would have been in territorial waters, registration would have been covered as described in the previous paragraph.

The *Marine Register of Deaths, 1855-1974 (GROS: MIN 10-45)* is the key series of records relating to deaths at sea of Scottish subjects. From 1975 onwards events are recorded in *the Consular and Foreign Records New Series: Combined Series (GROS: MIN 278 -)* The Marine Register of Deaths is subdivided into sections, namely:

| Date | Reference | Title | Description |
|------|-----------|-------|-------------|
| 1855-1874 | GROS: MIN 10-13 | Deaths: Intimations | Minutes, or copies of log book entries, sent by the captains of British merchant and Royal Navy ships directly to the GRO These should have been entered in the registers (GROS: MIN 16-19) |
| 1855-1893 | GROS: MIN 14-15 | Deaths: not registered | Probably informal notifications concerning deaths at sea received from individuals. |
| 1855-1876 | GROS: MIN 16-19 | Deaths: Register | Register of deaths at sea compiled from:<br>• Intimations (GROS: MIN 10-13)<br>• Reports of deaths aboard ships of any nationality carrying passengers to/from, the UK from/to places outside Europe |

| Date | Reference | Title | Description |
|------|-----------|-------|-------------|
| | | | and not within the Mediterranean<br>*Notes:*<br>• includes those joining the vessel within Europe etc.<br>• does not apply to territories under the jurisdiction of the East India Company (*see* footnote on page 100) |
| 1875-1974 | GROS: MIN 20-35 | Returns | Returns of deaths received from the RGSS; these should include events on:<br>• British merchant ships<br>• All non-British ships, with ports of departure or destination within the UK, carrying passengers |
| 1909-1974 | GROS: MIN 36-45 | Deaths: Printed returns | These probably duplicate material in the Deaths: Returns (GROS: MIN 20-35 above) but *see* note below. |

*Notes:* These regulations applied to all places where the laws of the United Kingdom applied. But, from 1894, they did not apply to dominion or colonial ships within the jurisdiction of the Government of the British possession to which they belonged.

Deaths on board vessels in territorial waters should be registered with the local Registrar of Deaths and so ought to be recorded in the general series of death registers but may not always have been.

From 1894 ships employed exclusively in trading between ports on the coasts of Scotland were exempt from the requirement to keep log books. It seems likely that any deaths were reported to a local registrar and thence to the GRO and RGSS. As most voyages would have been in territorial waters, registration would have been covered as described in the previous paragraph.

Whilst details of all deaths recorded on crew lists, prior to 1874, should have been reported directly to the GRO it would be unwise to rely on this. *See* note on equivalent English records above.

After 1894, particulars of deaths of merchant seamen who had been discharged sick, or who from other causes had recently left British vessels, would often have been recorded in the log book and in the registers of the RGSS. These entries would not have been reported to the GRO and so will not be found in these registers, though it is possible that they may be found in the set of Deaths: Printed Returns.

The various Acts do seem to require the same level of detail as called for when registering births or deaths that happened on land in Scotland, but this did not happen in practice. The forms filled in by masters only make provision for the rather more limited information required in England but, as will be seen from Figure 28, additional details obtained from the local registrar or from a relative might be added.

Indexes to these registers, separate from the general series, are available in the public search rooms of the GRO (Scotland) in Edinburgh and via the ScotLink terminal at the Family Records Centre in London, but these indexes do not seem to have been filmed by the LDS Church.[*] The indexes, to records over 50 years old for deaths and 100 years old for births may also be consulted on the web[†] at www.scotlandspeople.gov.uk where they form part of the Minor Records Index. Microfilm copies of the registers may be viewed in Edinburgh or certified copies of entries may be ordered on-line, by post or in person. Scanned images should also be available on-line soon.

---

[*] Neither are these indexes available in the Society of Genealogists library.

[†] The service previously available at www.scotsorigins.com/ ceased to operate from 1 September 2002 when it was transferred from Scots Origins to this site run by the GRO (Scotland) and Scotland On Line.

## Consular Registers (1914-date)

The GRO (Scotland) holds copies of registrations by British consuls relating to persons of Scottish descent or birth. Those for births date from 1914, deaths from 1925 and those for marriages from 1917; these are to be found in GROS: MIN 164 onwards. Earlier records will be found amongst those at the GRO (England and Wales).

As with their equivalents in England, these registers may contain details of births and deaths at sea of Scottish subjects. The marriage registers may also possibly contain details of marriages performed by Royal Naval captains acting within the terms of the Consular Marriage Acts.

In addition the GRO (Scotland) holds *High Commissioners' returns of death (from 1964)* and *Returns of births, deaths and marriages in foreign countries (1860-1965)*. The latter is based on information supplied by the parties concerned.

Indexes to these registers, separate from the general series, are available in the public search rooms of the GRO (Scotland) in Edinburgh and via the ScotLink terminal at the Family Records centre in London, but these indexes do not seem to have been filmed by the LDS Church.[*] The indexes, to records over 50 years old for deaths and 100 years old for births may also be consulted on the web[†] at www.scotlandspeople.gov.uk where they form part of the Minor Records Index. Microfilm copies of the registers may be viewed in Edinburgh or certified copies of entries may be ordered on-line, by post or in person. Scanned images should also be available on-line soon.

## Service Registers

It is unclear as to whether deaths of service personnel at sea would, from 1881 onwards, be recorded in the *Marine Deaths Register* or in one of the various service, or if appropriate war death registers, so it would be wise to check both.

---

[*]  Neither are these indexes available in the Society of Genealogists library.

[†]  The service previously available at www.scotsorigins.com/ ceased to operate from 1 September 2002 when it was transferred from Scots Origins to this site run by the GRO (Scotland) and Scotland On Line.

The GRO (Scotland) hold several series of registers that apply to service personnel, ordinarily resident in Scotland, recording events abroad and during war periods, namely:

| Period | Title | Comment |
|--------|-------|---------|
| 1883-1959 | Army [and other services] Returns of Births, Marriages and Deaths | • these relate to events abroad<br>• despite their name they do contain entries for all services |
| 1 April 1959-1974 | Service Department Registers of Births, Deaths and Marriages | • these relate to events abroad |
| 1899-1902 | Natal and South Africa War Deaths | |
| 1914-1918 | World War 1 Deaths | • covers both Army and Royal Navy<br>• does not included commissioned officers |
| 1939-1945 | World War 2 Deaths | • covers all the Armed Forces<br>• returns are incomplete |

*Note:* The missing returns for World Wars 1 and 2 will almost certainly be filled by the records at GRO (England and Wales) and at TNA.

There are also two registers of World War 1: Precognitions: US Army (MIN 147 and 148) in which are recorded deaths that took place when two troopships carrying US soldiers were lost off Islay. The *Tuscania* was sunk by a German submarine on 5 February 1918 and the *Otranto* was lost following a collision on 6 October 1918. Details of these are not included in the statutory index.

*Local registrars*
The Act under which civil registration was introduced in Scotland called for details of births and deaths at sea to be forwarded, by the GRO (Scotland), to the Registrar of the parish in which the child's parents, or the deceased, were last domiciled. An entry was then to be made in the local register. Under the above provisions details of births and deaths at sea should be recorded in local registers as well as in the Marine Registers at the GRO (Scotland). These records are not accessible to the public; all applications for information should be made through the GRO in Edinburgh.

# Ireland

## General

The key Acts in force at the time of the establishment of the Irish Free State in 1922 continued in force under the laws of the Republic of Ireland. Additionally reciprocal agreements regarding the exchange of information were made and some are still in operations. The reporting of deaths of Irish citizens to the GRO in Dublin by the UK authorities continues but those concerned with the reporting of the death of UK citizens aboard Irish vessels seem to have lapsed. So it is most convenient to describe the coverage of the marine registers once here and explain, under the headings of Dublin and Belfast, what each GRO holds.

It should be noted that the primary records at least should, from 1922, show a precise place of birth, not just Ireland, so that it could be determined to which GRO the report should be sent. If a place of birth, for a parent or deceased, was simply given as 'Ireland' then a return should have been made to both GROs.

## Marine Registers (1864-date)

The **Marine Register of Births, 1864- date** is the key series of records relating to births at sea of children with an Irish parent. The categories of events included are:

| From | Categories included: | Applicability |
|------|----------------------|---------------|
| 1864 | Births taking place on a British vessel where one of the parents was an Irish subject. | • Royal Navy ships<br>• British merchant ships<br>These consist of certified copies of minutes, or copies of log book entries, sent by the captains of British merchant and Royal Navy ships directly to the GRO. |
| 1864 | Births, to an Irish-born parent, taking place on board ships carrying passengers to/from UK. | • Ships carry passengers to/from, the UK from/to places outside Europe and not within the Mediterranean<br>*Notes:*<br>• includes those joining the vessel within Europe etc.<br>• does not apply to territories under the jurisdiction of the East India Company (*see* footnote on page 100) |

| From | Categories included: | Applicability |
|---|---|---|
| 1875 | Births taking place on board where the father or, if the child was a bastard, the mother, was Irish-born. | • Royal Navy ships<br>• British merchant ships<br>• All non-British ships, with ports of departure or destination within the UK, carrying passengers<br><br>These consist of returns made by the RGSS, for merchant vessels, and by the captains of Royal Navy vessels. |

*Notes:* These regulations applied to all places where the laws of the United Kingdom applied. But, from 1894, they did not apply to dominion or colonial ships within the jurisdiction of the Government of the British possession to which they belonged.

Births on board vessels in territorial waters should be registered with the local Registrar of Births and so ought to be recorded in the general series of birth registers but may not always have been.

The *Marine Register of Deaths, 1864-date* is the key series of records relating to deaths at sea of Irish persons. The categories of events included are:

| From | Categories included: | Applicability |
|---|---|---|
| 1 January 1864 | Deaths of Irish-born persons taking place on a British vessel | • Royal Navy ships<br>• British merchant ships<br>*Note:* These requirements may have been interpreted not to cover crew – *see* note below.<br><br>These consist of certified copies of minutes, or copies of log book entries, sent by the captains of British merchant and Royal Navy ships directly to the GRO. |

| From | Categories included: | Applicability |
|------|----------------------|---------------|
| 1 January 1864 | Deaths, of Irish-born persons, taking place on board ships carrying passengers to/from UK | • Ships carry passengers to/from, the UK from /to places outside Europe and not within the Mediterranean<br><br>*Notes:*<br>  • includes those joining the vessel within Europe etc.<br>  • does not apply to territories under the jurisdiction of the East India Company (*see* footnote on page 100) |
| 1875 | Deaths taking place on board where the deceased was Irish-born. | • Royal Navy ships<br>• British merchant ships<br>• All non-British ships, with ports of departure or destination within the UK, carrying passengers<br><br>These consist of returns made by the RGSS, for merchant vessels, and by the captains of Royal Navy vessels. |

*Notes:* These regulations applied to all places where the laws of the United Kingdom applied. But, from 1894, they did not apply to dominion or colonial ships within the jurisdiction of the Government of the British possession to which they belonged.

Deaths on board vessels in territorial waters should be registered with the local Registrar of Deaths and so ought to be recorded in the general series of death registers but may not always have been.

Whilst details of all deaths recorded on crew lists, prior to 1874, should have been reported directly to the GRO it would be unwise to rely on this.

After 1894, particulars of deaths of merchant seamen who had been discharged sick, or who from other causes had recently left British vessels, would often have been recorded in the log book and in the registers of the RGSS. These entries would not have been reported to the GRO and so will not be found in these registers.

*Dublin*

Marine Registers

The records held by the GRO in Dublin are for:

- Births of children at sea where one of the parents was Irish, registered from 1 January 1864 to 31 December 1921;

- Births of children at sea (on British or Irish ships) where one of the parents was born in the Republic of Ireland, registered from 1 January 1922;

- Deaths at sea of Irish-born persons, registered from 1 January 1864 to 31 December 1921;

- Deaths at sea of Irish-born persons (on British or Irish ships), other than those born in Northern Ireland, registered from 1 January 1864 to 31 December 1921.

From 1886 onwards there are printed indexes bound into the back of the general annual indexes to births and deaths. These indexes are available in the public search rooms of the GRO in both Dublin and Belfast (deaths on microfilm), and on microfilm through a LDS Family History Library.[*] The indexes to earlier registers must be requested from the staff at the GRO.

Other records

The GRO in Dublin also holds some other sets of registers that may possibly contain reference to events at sea as explained above in the section for England and Wales. These are:

- Registers of Births of children of Irish parents, certified by British Consuls abroad, from 1 January 1864 to 31 December 1921.

  There are no indexes to these registers, which are small; they must be requested from the staff in the public search room.

- Registers of Deaths of Irish-born persons, certified by British Consuls abroad, from 1 January 1864 to 31 December 1921.

  There are no indexes to these registers, which are small; they must be requested from the staff in the public search room.

- Registers under the Births, Deaths and Marriages (Army) Act 1879.

---

[*]  These indexes are not available in the Society of Genealogists library.

These apply to Irish subjects serving in the British army abroad. Separate indexes are bound into the back of each main annual volume, beginning in 1888 and continuing to 1930 (for births) and 1931 (marriages and deaths). The death index for 1902 also includes an index to 'Deaths of Irish subjects pertaining to the South African War (1898-1902)'. These indexes are available in the public search rooms of the GROs both in Dublin and Belfast (deaths on microfilm) and on microfilm through a LDS Family History Library*.

## Belfast

### Marine Registers

The records held by the GRO in Belfast all relate to events registered from 1 January 1922. They apply to:

- Births of children at sea on British-registered ships where one parents was Irish, and gave an address that was not in the Republic of Ireland (namely was in Northern Ireland or simply said Ireland);

- Deaths at sea of Irish-born persons on British-registered ships, other than those born in Republic of Ireland (namely was in Northern Ireland or simply said Ireland).

These registers are compiled from returns made by the RGSS and the commanding officers of Royal Navy ships; none relate to events on ships registered in the Republic of Ireland.

The GRO in Belfast hold both paper and computerised indexes to births and deaths from 1922. They also hold copies of the printed birth and death indexes (on microfilm for deaths) for the period 1864-1921 which include events for the whole of Ireland as described above under Dublin.

### Other records

The GRO in Belfast also holds some other sets of registers that may possibly contain reference to events at sea as explained above in the section for England and Wales. These are:

- Registers of Births of children of Northern Ireland parents, certified by British Consuls abroad, from 1 January 1922;

---

*  These indexes are not available in the Society of Genealogists library.

- Registers of Deaths of Northern Irish persons, certified by British Consuls abroad, from 1 January 1922;

- High Commissioners' returns of births, deaths and marriages of Northern Ireland persons, registered by British High Commissioners in Commonwealth countries after 1 January 1950;

- Service Department Registers: Records of births of children whose father was born in Northern Ireland, deaths and marriages registered after 1 January 1922 under the Births, Deaths and Marriages (Army) Act 1879.

  These apply to persons serving in the British army abroad. Separate indexes are bound into the back of each main annual volume, beginning in 1888 and continuing to 1930 (for births) and 1931 (marriages and deaths). The death index for 1902 also includes an index to 'Deaths of Irish subjects pertaining to the South African War (1898-1902)'. These indexes are available in the public search rooms of the GROs both in Dublin and Belfast (deaths on microfilm) and on microfilm through a LDS Family History Library.

- War Deaths of persons born in Northern Ireland who died on war service between 1929 and 1948.

Indexes to all these series of registers should be available in the public search rooms of the GRO in Belfast.

**Colonial**

A number of colonial administrations made provision, within their system of civil registration, for the recording of events that took place at sea. It is beyond the scope of a modest-sized book such as this to attempt to survey them all. But below we have summarised details of some about which we have information.

*Australia*
General
Civil registration in Australia is organised on a state and territory basis and this is discussed below. There are though a few general points to make.

Death registrations for service personnel killed overseas during the South African (Boer) Wars and later are not held by the state registries but by the relevant service to which applications for certificates should be directed (*see* Appendix 4, Useful Addresses).

Registrations for Australian citizens lodged overseas at embassies, consulates, high commissions etc are not held by the state registries. These are the responsibility of the Department of Immigration and Multicultural Affairs to which application should be made for records more recent than 30 years old (*see* Appendix 4, Useful Addresses). Older records are available at the National Archives, in Canberra – fuller details are available in their Fact Sheet 89 available from their website (www.naa.gov.au).

## New South Wales

When civil registration was introduced into New South Wales, on 1 March 1856, provision was made for the recording of births and deaths that occurred at sea whilst en route to NSW. The returns include, in addition to the name of the person, the name of the ship, its port of origin and the latitude and longitude where the event took place.

Marine births and deaths were originally bound into separate registers and given a number beginning with an 'M'. Marine births (from 1888) and marine deaths (from 1894) were recorded on separate sheets but bound up with the ordinary returns at the end of each year and allocated a number in sequence with the other births and deaths.

The obligation to register any marriage performed by him on the voyage rested with the clergyman. Marriages could not legally be performed by the master of the vessel.

Three indexes to events registered in New South Wales have been published both on microfiche and on CD-ROM, namely:

- NSW Pioneers Index 1788-1888
- NSW Federation Index 1889-1918
- NSW Between the Wars 1919-1945

These index all birth (up to 1918), death (to 1945) and marriage (to 1945) records held by the NSW Registry. Included also are baptisms, burials, and marriages, recorded in local church registers before the introduction of state-wide civil registration in 1856, for which the NSW Registry hold registers.

The indexes to births (to 1905), deaths (to 1945) and marriages (to 1945) may be searched on line at www.bdm.nsw.gov.au/. These do index births and marriages at sea – with a registration district of 'Marine'.

112

Certificates for these events should be requested from the NSW Registry of Births, Deaths and Marriages in Sydney.

The Australian Vital Records Index (VRI)[*], published by the LDS on CD-ROM, includes births, deaths and marriages registered in NSW, 1788-1888; deaths at sea, 1788-1888, are indexed there.

## Victoria

When civil registration was introduced into Victoria, on 1 July 1853, provision was made for the recording of births, deaths and marriages that occurred on ships arriving at Victorian ports. There are separate marine registers up to 1872; from 1873 onwards such events are recorded in the general series. For events taking place at sea the registration number will include the letter 'M'.

Several indexes to events registered in Victoria have been published both on microfiche and on CD-ROM, namely:

- Victorian Pioneers Index 1836-1888
- Victorian Federation Index 1889-1901
- Victorian Edwardian Index 1902-1913
- Victorian Great War Index 1914-1920
- Victorian Marriage Index 1921-1942
- Victorian Death Index 1921-1985

These index all records of birth, death and marriage (except as indicated otherwise by the title) held by the Victorian Registry. Included also are baptisms, burials, and marriages recorded in local church registers before the introduction of state-wide civil registration in 1853, for which they hold registers. Certificates for these events should be requested from the Victorian Registry of Births, Deaths and Marriages in Melbourne.

The indexes to births (to 1924), deaths (to 1985) and marriages (to 1939) may be searched on line at www.justice.vic.gov.au/.

---

[*] The Australian VRI is not available inside Australia, and the accuracy of its contents should be treated with a little caution.

The Australian Vital Records Index (VRI)[*], published by the LDS on CD-ROM, includes births, deaths and marriages registered in Victoria, 1837-1888. Births, deaths and marriages at sea are indexed there. The Australian VRI contains several hundred marriage entries, recorded in the Victorian registry, for which it gives the place of marriage as 'at sea' but the vast majority of these did not actually take place at sea. It would seem as if, during the indexing process where one of the parties gave a place of birth as 'at sea', this has appeared in this index as being the place of marriage. A similar misinterpretation of the data has also occurred with deaths. In many instances where the VRI shows the place of death as 'at sea' the actual registers record that the deceased's place of birth as 'at sea'. If the event actually took place at sea the registration number will include the letter 'M'.

A CD-ROM specifically covering *Marine Births, Deaths and Marriages, Victoria, 1853-1920* has been published. This contains both an index and scanned images of the original entries in the Marine Register and of entries in the general registers referring to events at sea. There are only some three entries of marriages recorded on this CD-ROM: all of these have been extracted from the general series of registers.

Queensland

Compulsory registration of births, deaths and marriages began in Queensland, when it was part of NSW, on 1 March 1856 and continued following separation in December 1859. So far the Registrar-General has released indexes to these records for births (up to 1919), marriages (to 1939) and deaths (to 1954); all of these indexes are available on microfiche.

Two indexes to events registered in Queensland have been published on microfiche and on CD-ROM, namely:

- Queensland Pioneers Index 1829-1889

- Queensland Federation Index 1890-1914

These index all births, deaths and marriages registered following the start of civil registration in 1856. They cover also those church records of baptisms and burials (starting in 1829) and marriage (starting in 1839), later acquired by the Queensland Registry.

---

[*]  The Australian VRI is not available inside Australia, and the accuracy of its contents should be treated with a little caution.

For events occurring after 1889, application for certificates should be made to the Queensland Registry of Births, Deaths and Marriages in Brisbane. Earlier records are held by Queensland State Archives.

The Australian Vital Records Index, published by the LDS on CD-ROM does not cover Queensland.

Under the civil registration system, births and deaths at sea were registered in Queensland and there are separate indexes to them. Registration numbers for events at sea will contain the letters 'MA'.

## South Australia

Compulsory registration of births, deaths and marriages began in South Australia on 1 July 1842. Indexes are available, on CD-ROM for births (1842-1906) deaths (1842-1915) and marriages (1842-1937). These are continued on microfiche for births (1907-1922), deaths (1916-1970) and marriages (1917-1937). Applications for certificates should be made to the South Australian Registry of Births, Deaths and Marriages in Adelaide.

The Australian Vital Records Index, published by the LDS on CD-ROM does not cover South Australia.

Births at sea, to parents normally residing in South Australia, may be found recorded in the South Australian registry system. In addition, although not civil registration records, there are two useful sources:

- Register of Deaths at Sea, 1893-1922
  These seem to relate to Port Adelaide and are held by the South Australian Regional Office of the National Archives of Australia (reference CRS D7)

- Return of Persons who Died on Board Emigrant Ships, 1849 to 5 June 1865, published in the *South Australian Government Gazette* of 25 January 1866 pages 75-96.* This records the deaths of those on ships arriving in South Australia giving details.

---

\* A copy is available at TNA in PRO CO 16/20.

## Western Australia

Compulsory registration of births, deaths and marriages began in Western Australia on 9 September 1841.

An index is available, both on microfiche and on CD-ROM, (*Western Australia Pioneers Index, 1841-1905*) covering all three events for that time period. The Australian Vital Records Index (VRI),[*] published by the LDS on CD-ROM, also includes births, deaths and marriages registered in Western Australia, 1841-1905; births and death at sea, are correctly indexed there. These indexes are continued on microfiche for deaths (1906-1980) and marriages (1906-1965). Applications for certificates should be made to the Western Australian Registry of Births, Deaths and Marriages in Perth.

Masters of British and colonial ships on arrival at any port in the State were responsible for informing the District Registrar of any births or deaths that had occurred at sea.[83] The Western Australian Registry holds *Marine Registers of Births and Deaths* in which these are recorded.

In addition, although not civil registration records, the State Records Office of Western Australia holds some records of births and deaths at sea reported in Western Australian ports. These records were created by the Harbour and Light Department:

- Register of Births (1902-1915) and Deaths (1902-1917) off the Western Australian coast (reference: Acc 1056, Item 63, WAS 1618).

- Register - Births (1918-1921) and Deaths (1917-1964) at Sea (reference: Acc 1316, Item 19, AN 16).

- Returns Respecting Seamen - Discharged, Deserted, Dead, 1914-1966 (reference: Acc 1316, Item 5, AN 16).

- Records of Shipping Casualties, 1905-1916 (reference: Acc 1056, Item 61, WAS 1618).

## Tasmania

Compulsory registration of births, deaths and marriages began in Tasmania on 1 December 1838.

---

[*] The Australian VRI is not available inside Australia, and the accuracy of its contents should be treated with a little caution.

An index is available on CD-ROM (*Tasmanian Pioneers Index, 1803-1899*) covering all three events for that time period. Included also are baptisms, burials, and marriages, recorded in local church registers before the introduction of state-wide civil registration in 1838, for which the Tasmanian Registry hold registers. Copies of the pre-1900 records are available on microfilm. Applications for later certificates should be made to the Tasmanian Registry of Births, Deaths and Marriages in Hobart.

The Australian Vital Records Index (VRI),[*] published by the LDS on CD-ROM, includes births, deaths and marriages registered in Tasmania 1803-1899; no events at sea are to be found there.

These indexes are continued on microfiche for:

- deaths and marriages (1900-1914)

- births (1900-1905) and deaths and marriages (1915-1919)

### Northern Territory
Civil registration of births, deaths and marriages began in the Northern Territory on 24 August 1870; prior to that date events were registered under the South Australian civil registration system. Indexes are available on microfiche for births (to 1918), deaths (to 1913) and marriages (to 1913). Certified copies of entries are available from the Registry. Children born at sea of parents who were residents of the Northern Territory could be registered up to nine months after arrival of the child in the Northern Territory[84].

The Australian Vital Records Index, published by the LDS on CD-ROM does not cover either the Northern Territory or South Australia.

---

[*] The Australian VRI is not available inside Australia, and the accuracy of its contents should be treated with a little caution.

## Australian Capital Territory

Records of civil registration in ACT date from 1 January 1930; prior to that date registration of any events would have been recorded in the NSW system. Although ACT technically has a seaport (Jervis Bay) it has never been developed and it seems extremely unlikely that any events taking place at sea would have been candidates for registration under the system of that otherwise land-locked territory.

## *New Zealand*

Civil registration, for Europeans, began in New Zealand in 1848 but was not made compulsory until 1856. The 19th century registers do contain some entries where the birth of a child was registered in the general registration system on arrival in New Zealand. But in most cases births, deaths or marriages were recorded only in the ship's log or other papers; these records may be found at Archives New Zealand.

The Births and Deaths Registration Act 1951 made provision for the registration of births and deaths that occurred outside New Zealand on a New Zealand registered ship. There are no separate registers for these events; entries are included in the general system.

Microfiche copies of the indexes are available to 1990.

## *South Africa*

In colonial times there was no central system of registration of births or deaths amongst whites; this was based on the individual colonies and provinces. These systems began in Natal in 1868, Cape Province in 1895, Transvaal in 1901, Orange Free State in 1902 and South-West Africa in 1913. It is not known whether any special provision was made for the registration of births or deaths en route to South Africa, but this seems unlikely. Certificates from these registries can be obtained from the South African Department of Home Affairs; for those applying from overseas this should be made through the nearest South African Mission or Consulate – fuller details are given on their website at www.home-affairs.gov.za/. This avenue is of limited use since the indexes are not publicly available and an application must contain more information than the average researcher is likely to have. A number of the registers have, though, been filmed and are available through LDS Family History Libraries - they are to be found in their catalogue (available on line at www.familysearch.org) under South Africa: Civil Registration.

*Other former colonies*

The legislation[85] of a number of former colonies makes some specific provision related to the recording of events taking place aboard ship. Those noted there are:

- Bahamas (births and deaths)
- British Honduras (births and deaths)
- Gold Coast and Togoland (births and deaths)
- Malta – to exclude recording of deaths of persons belonging to the Royal Navy or any foreign navy under certain conditions.
- Nigeria and the Cameroons (births and deaths)
- Singapore (births and deaths)

## United States of America

The US Department of Health and Human Services[86] advises that when a birth or death occurs on the high seas, the record is usually filed at the next port of call.

- If the vessel docked at a foreign port, requests for copies of the record may be made to the US Department of State, Washington, DC 20522-1705.

- If the first port of entry was in the United States, write to the registration authority in the city where the vessel docked in the United States.

- If the vessel was of US registry, contact the local authorities at the port of entry and/or search the vessel logs at the US Coast Guard Facility at the vessel's final port of call for that voyage.

## Note added in press:

As the book was going to press the authors became aware of two additional useful series of documents. The National Archives of Australia, Western Australia Regional Office (PO Box 1144, East Victoria Park, WA 6981) holds:

- Register of births, deaths and marriages at sea, 1922-1938 (PP174/3 volume 1).
- Correspondence records: Deaths at sea, 1922-1946 (PT1804/1) consisting of 87 files alphabetically arranged and indexed by name in their on-line catalogue at www.naa.gov.au.

Births on board the British Barque [Shah?]
of London on a voyage from London to Halifax
in Nova Scotia & Jamaica to London.

| When Name Sex Name of Father | Name & maiden name of Mother of Father | Rank, profession of Father | Signature of Master |
|---|---|---|---|
| N° 24 | [illegible] None | Girl Rob.t Tattock | Maria Tattock formerly Brook | Jas Strand Master |

Laid Nov.r 18th 1839. at Halifax. Nova Sc[otia]

a true copy. [White]

Registrar General.

Figure 26: An early entry in the Marine Register of Births, England and Wales

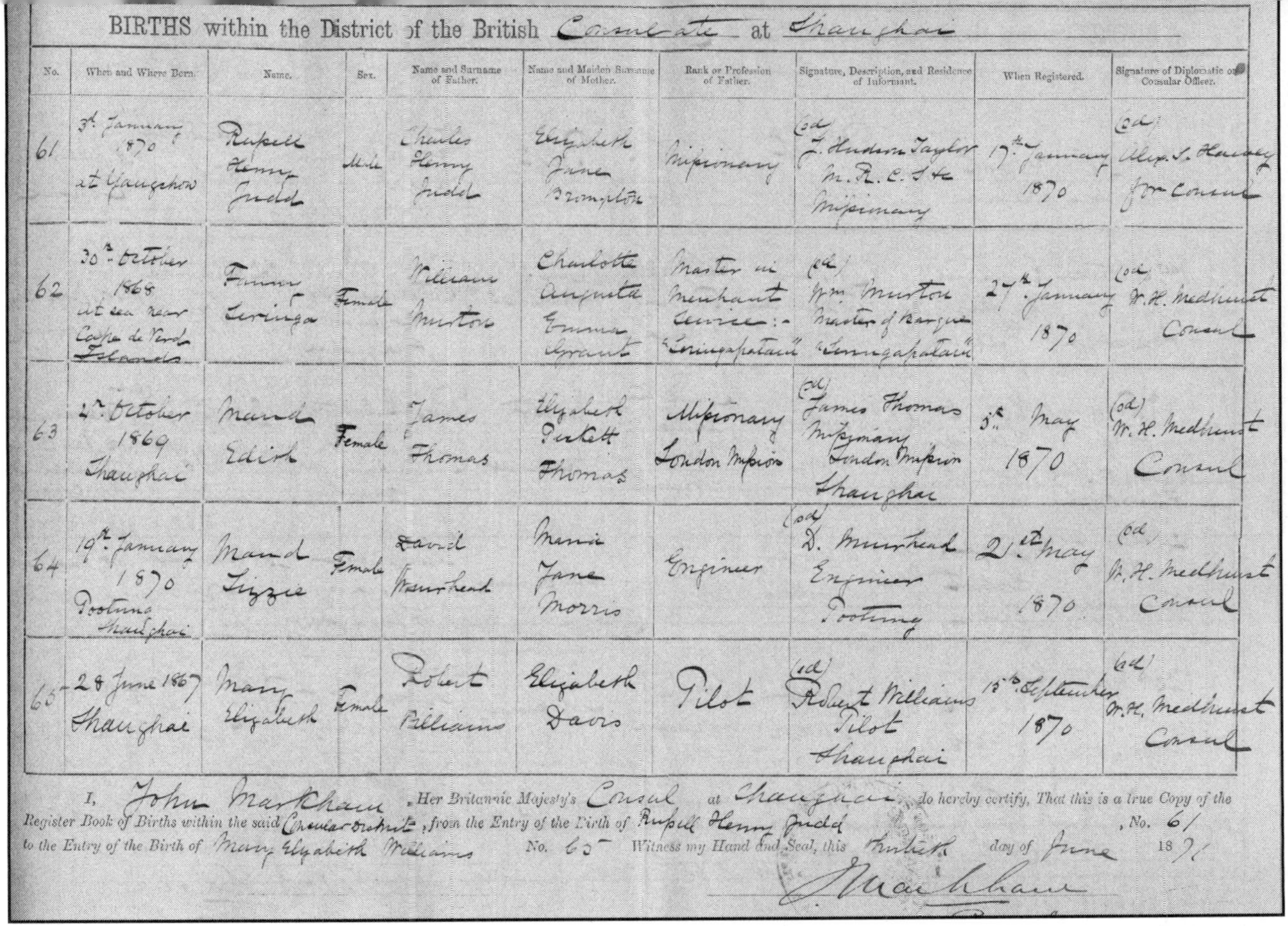

BIRTHS within the District of the British Consulate at Shanghai

| No. | When and Where Born. | Name. | Sex. | Name and Surname of Father. | Name and Maiden Surname of Mother. | Rank or Profession of Father. | Signature, Description, and Residence of Informant. | When Registered. | Signature of Diplomatic or Consular Officer. |
|---|---|---|---|---|---|---|---|---|---|
| 61 | 3rd January 1870 at Yangchow | Russell Henry Judd | Male | Charles Henry Judd | Elizabeth Jane Brompton | Missionary | (sd) J. Hudson Taylor M.R.C.S &c Missionary | 17th January 1870 | (sd) Alex. S. Harvey for Consul |
| 62 | 30th October 1868 at sea near Cape de Verd Islands | Fanny Seringa | Female | William Murton | Charlotte Augusta Emma Grant | Master in Merchant Service:- "Seringapatam" | (sd) Wm Murton Master of Barque "Seringapatam" | 27th January 1870 | (sd) W. H. Medhurst Consul |
| 63 | 4th October 1869 Shanghai | Maud Edith | Female | James Thomas | Elizabeth Puckett Thomas | Missionary London Mission | (sd) James Thomas Missionary London Mission Shanghai | 5th May 1870 | (sd) W. H. Medhurst Consul |
| 64 | 19th January 1870 Pootung Shanghai | Maud Lizzie | Female | David Muirhead | Maria Jane Morris | Engineer | (sd) D. Muirhead Engineer Pootung | 21st May 1870 | (sd) W. H. Medhurst Consul |
| 65 | 28 June 1867 Shanghai | Mary Elizabeth | Female | Robert Williams | Elizabeth Davis | Pilot | (sd) Robert Williams Pilot Shanghai | 15th September 1870 | (sd) W. H. Medhurst Consul |

I, John Markham, Her Britannic Majesty's Consul at Shanghai do hereby certify, That this is a true Copy of the Register Book of Births within the said Consular District, from the Entry of the Birth of Russell Henry Judd, No. 61 to the Entry of the Birth of Mary Elizabeth Williams No. 65 Witness my Hand and Seal, this thirtieth day of June 1871

J. Markham

*Figure 27: Birth at sea recorded in the Shanghai consular registers (PRO FO 681/1 f.120)*

Page

**MARINE REGISTER OF DEATHS.**

| No. | DESCRIPTION OF THE DECEASED. | | | | | | |
|---|---|---|---|---|---|---|---|
| | Name, Rank, Profession, or Occupation, and Usual Residence. | Sex. | Age. | Where born. | Parents' Names, and Rank, Profession, or Occupation. | If Deceased was married, To whom. | Issue, in Order of Birth, their Names and Age |
| 1. | Scotland James<br>Private | Male | 27<br>Years | Parish of<br>Tulliallan,<br>County of Perth | William Scotland<br>Sea Captain (Deceased)<br>Jane Scotland,<br>Maiden name Donald | | |

| PARTICULARS OF DEATH. | | | | | |
|---|---|---|---|---|---|
| When died. Year, Day of Month, Hour. | Where died. Name of Vessel, and Latitude and Longitude to be stated. | Cause of Death, and how long Disease continued. Medical Attendant by whom certified, and when he last saw deceased. | Burial Place. Undertaker by whom certified. | Signature, Designation, and Usual Residence of Informant. | When and where registered, and Signature of Registrar-General. |
| 1855.<br>January Fifth<br>10h. A.M. | On board the<br>"Candia"<br>(British Vessel) | Dysentery<br>(Not certified) | At Sea<br>(Not certified) | (Signed) James Edward Field,<br>Commander of the "Candia"<br>(Some of the particulars furnished by the Registrar of Tulliallan) | 1855,<br>January 29th<br>At Edinburgh<br>W. P. Dundas<br>Registrar General |

*Figure 28: First entry in the Marine Register of Deaths, Scotland*

# SUBSIDIARY SOURCES

## Introduction

So far we have concentrated on sources whose prime purpose was to record births, deaths and marriages at sea. Here we will look somewhat wider at a range of subsidiary sources that may incidentally make mention of these events. The purpose in doing so is twofold. Firstly they may be the only source that makes mention of the event due to the lack of primary source material. Secondly they may provide a necessary clue that will make the search for primary source material a practical proposition by narrowing its scope, for example in time or by identifying the vessel on which the event took place.

Clearly the range of material is potentially unlimited so we will concentrate on that which has helped us in our past searches. Also we will only briefly identify such items and not discuss them in any depth; wherever possible we will refer to published guides wherein fuller details may be found.

## Occupational records

An overview of much of the material identified below is to be found *in Tracing Your Ancestors in the PRO*.[87]

### Merchant seamen
Considerable quantities of records survive related to the registration of merchant seamen (1835 1857 and 1918-1972) and for the granting of certificates to merchant sea officers (1845-1969). Although the earlier seamen's registers (1835-1857) rarely make mention of deaths at sea, the later ones and those for officers often do so. Most of this material is to be found at TNA and there is a comprehensive guide to it.[88]

The entries in *Lloyd's Captain's Register* (1869-1948) are likely in many instances to note when an officer had died. The originals of these records are at the Guildhall Library in London and have been microfilmed. The annually published *Mercantile Navy List* contains, for the period 1857-1864, what it terms as obituaries of those with master's certificates; these usually simply record place and date of death.

Prior to the Merchant Shipping Act of 1854, the Corporation of Trinity House had at its disposal certain charitable funds for the benefit of seafarers and their dependants throughout the UK, independent of any previous connection with Trinity House. In order to benefit from these a seafarer (mostly mercantile mariners) or his dependants had to make application to Trinity House. This application took the form of a Petition, which gave details of his circumstances and often seafaring career. A number of these make mention of the deaths at sea of seafaring husbands or fathers, for example:

---

**To the Honorable the Master, Wardens *and* Assistants, of the CORPORATION of TRINITY-HOUSE of Deptford-Strond.**

**The humble Petition**
of *Emily Darnell*
aged *Thirty four* Years, residing
at *Great Yarmouth*
Widow of *Thomas Darnell*

**Sheweth,** THAT your Petitioner's Husband went to Sea at the age of *Ten* in the Year *1827* and has been employed in the Merchant Sea Service for *24* Years, in the following Ships, and others, in the annexed Stations:

...

That your Petitioner's Husband ~~left off the~~ *was lost at* Sea in the Year *1851* in ~~consequence of~~ *the Gale of the 25ᵗʰ Sept* ~~and died~~ _____ and she has *5* children, viz. *2* Boys under 12 Years of Age, and *3* Girls under 14 Years of Age, viz.

...

---

Thomas Darnell's death is not recorded in the *Marine Deaths Register* for England and Wales. The only possibilities to be found in general series were for events registered in inland districts.

These records suffered badly by fire in 1666 and 1714; those that now survive cover the period 1787-1854. The original *Trinity House Petitions*, bound up in two alphabetical series, previously at the Society of Genealogists, are now at the Guildhall Library:

| | | |
|---|---|---|
| Ms 30218A | Main series of petitions | 1787-1854 |
| Ms 30218B | Second series of petitions | 1787-1853 |

The records are available at both locations on microfilm; both series are indexed in the published Trinity House Petitions.[89]

Records of service in the Royal Naval Reserve (RNR) are available at TNA and may make mention of deaths of men in service. Those for officers, serving between 1862 and 1920, are in series ADM 240; later material is still with the Ministry of Defence. The records in series ADM 340 do also include RNR officers, covering those with dates of birth prior to 1900, but may well duplicate much that is to be found in ADM 240. Samples of records for seamen, serving up to 1913, are in BT 164; after that date all the records have been preserved in BT 377. Records of those who served in the Trawler Section seem to have been included, irrespective of rank, in BT 377.

*Royal Navy*

Comprehensive registers and records of service survive, mostly at TNA, and these are likely to make mention of any deaths in service. The arrangement of this material depends on whether the man was a commissioned officer, warrant officer or rating. Discussion of this is far beyond the scope of this book and the searcher should consult the two more detailed works[90] on the subject. Material is normally available for ratings who joined up to 1923, for warrant officers to 1931 and executive offices to May 1917; later material is with the Ministry of Defence.

Records of both officers and ratings in the Royal Naval Volunteer Reserve (RNVR), 1914-1918, are at TNA in PRO series ADM 337; later material is with the Ministry of Defence.

The Admiralty actively encouraged seamen to write wills and the survival of this material is described below.

*Royal Marines*

The Royal Marines kept their own registers of baptisms, burials and marriages and these have already been described in the chapter on Admiralty records. Records of service, for both officers, commissioned up to 1922, and marines who enlisted up to 1923 are available; later material is with the Ministry of Defence. A guide to these records has been published.[91]

*Civil Servants*

The record series *Civil Service Commission: Evidences of Age, 1855-1939* contains details of the births of candidates for appointment to the Civil Service. The files include persons born between approximately 1820 and 1900; many examples are to be found where the individual was born at sea. These records, formerly at TNA in series CSC 1, are now at the Society of Genealogists and an index to them is being prepared for publication. It is perhaps wrong to consider these just as subsidiary sources since they do contain many declarations made by parents concerning the date and place of birth of their child and thus might be considered as a primary source, even though written many years after the event. Often they record information either not to be found elsewhere, or else needing to be gleaned from multiple sources. The following two examples illustrate these points.

Amongst these records is to be found the following declaration, dated 6 May 1875:

> I *James Quigley*
> *Quartermaster Sergeant, 10th Brigade Depot Barracks, Bradford, Yorkshire*
> do solemnly and sincerely declare that *my son*
> *Alexander Quigley was born at sea on board the Troop-ship Sevilla when near the Island of Madeira on the 3rd day of November 1860*

This is supported by a baptismal certificate showing that Alexander, child of James and Jane Quigley, born 3 November 1860, was baptised at St Paul's Church, Auckland, New Zealand on 2 June 1861; the father's occupation is given as Serjeant, 14th Regt, abode Camp Otahuhu.

This birth is not recorded in the GRO (England and Wales)'s *Index to Marine Births*. It is though recorded in the *Registers of Births, Deaths and Marriages of Passengers at Sea (BT 158/2)* simply as a male child of Jane Quigley born 3 Novr 1860 aboard the ship *Sevilla* (ON 27737). A record submitted by an LDS Church member, and included in the IGI, claims that this individual was born 3 November 1860 in Auckland. The *Sevilla* carried men of the 2nd Bttn 14th Foot to New Zealand leaving London on 5 November 1860 reaching Queenstown on 16 October 1860 and arriving in Auckland on 25 February 1861.[92]

Alexander Quigley, whose occupation then was a telegraphist, is listed together with his parents and siblings, in the 1881 census for Bradford.[93] This reinforces the oft-repeated advice to check information from several sources.

The contents of the files must be read with care. Amongst the papers filed related to the birth of George McNabb is what, at first glance, appears to be a birth certificate. On more careful examination, it will be found that it is actually a request from the Civil Service Commission for a search to be made at the General Register Office but it gives all the information that one might expect to find on a birth certificate. On the reverse of it are to be found the words 'Not returned to G.R.O. application had better be made to the Reg$^r$ Gen$^l$ of Shipping & Seamen...' No note is made as to the result of that search, but the details are supported by a declaration, dated 28 January 1879:

> I *Ann McNabb, residing at 28, Old Park Road, Belfast and mother of George McNabb*
> do solemnly and sincerely declare that *he was born on the 4$^{th}$ day of August 1860 on board the British Barque "Elizabeth" in Latitude 40°S and Longitude 138°W.*

## Baptisms and burials

It should be remembered that although a birth may have taken place aboard a ship, the baptism of the child may have not have been performed until the ship reached an appropriate port. The entry of baptism might be the only record relating to the birth of the child or might provide a clue that will help locate any surviving record. Registers at port cities must surely contain more than the average for such events.

In addition, it is worth looking in the International Genealogical Index (IGI) which has a separate section for events that occurred 'At Sea'.

Burial registers of coastal parishes do sometimes contain information on shipwrecks recording the names of the ships and their crew, where known, even if the bodies were never found.

## Graves and memorials

Gravestones and memorials in churchyards and cemeteries do not always restrict themselves to mentioning those buried under or near the stone. There are numerous examples where family members buried elsewhere, on land or at sea, or even just lost at sea are commemorated. For example a tombstone in the churchyard of St Anne, Limehouse, Middlesex includes the words:[94]

.. also Mr Richard James Jenney, barrister at law, son in law of the above [i.e. Mr James Hall], who died at sea on his passage to Trinidad Feb 25th 1838, aged 44 [possibly 41] years...

The Commonwealth War Graves Commission (CWGC) holds details about Royal Navy personnel and merchant seamen who died on ships during both World Wars, and civilian war dead for World War 2. They may be buried in a grave or one of the very many war cemeteries around the world. Where there is no known grave then the CWGC holds details of memorials on which their name may be commemorated. For instance those from the merchant navy and fishing fleets, who gave their lives during the two World Wars, and were either lost or buried at sea and have no known grave are commemorated on the Tower Hill Memorial and the Halifax Memorial. The best way to access this information is from the CWGC website at www.cwgc.org, which includes an on-line searchable register. These registers should yield the date and place of death (ship).

Servicemen and women, including those in the Merchant Navy and Merchant Fleet Auxiliary, who died during World War 1 are listed in the five volumes of the Cross of Sacrifice.[95] The information it contains is based on the Commonwealth War Register.

Churchyards in coastal parishes do sometimes contain monuments to ships lost, recording the names of the crew where known. The National Maritime Museum has, for a long time, been compiling a record of monuments to people connected with the sea.[96] For Royal Navy personnel then a search of local war memorials may help.

## Wills

The Wills, or Letters of Administration, of those dying at sea after 12 January 1858 with property in England and Wales should be included in the normal series of probate records. Prior to 1858, jurisdiction over those dying at sea rested with the Prerogative Court of Canterbury (PCC), thus a search amongst their records may prove fruitful.[97] The indexes, of which many have been published and some are online, are quite helpful in that they usually name the ship, say 'at sea' or 'Parts' (meaning died in foreign parts). All of the register copies of PCC wills, in series PROB 11, (1384-1858) are available on line at www.documentsonline.pro.gov.uk and an index to PCC wills (1750-1800) is also available at www.englishorigins.com. Inventories of those who died at sea, and left a will proved in the PCC (1661-1720), are covered by a card index to TNA series PROB 4 available in their reading rooms.

After 1815 the possibility of proving the will of a seamen in the PCC only remained if he was owed more then £20 in wages otherwise these had to be proved in a local probate court. Anthony Camp[98] points out that, from the mid-18th century onwards, most local probate courts contain some wills of people dying at sea or overseas.

The records of two London courts, both of whose records are at the Guildhall Library, are also rich in wills for mariners dying overseas. The underlying reason behind this is discussed in Anthony Camp's article (*loc cit*) and in the introduction to Marc Fitch's *Index to Testamentary Records in the Archdeaconry Court of London.*[99] Those records for the Commissary Court of London (London Division) include many wills of merchant seamen from the late 17th century to 1857. The Archdeaconry Court of London also contains numerous records of mariners, many of whom were ascribed as having residences in London parishes, often St Botolph Aldgate. The records of this latter court cease in 1807. Many indexes to wills proved in these two courts have been published and those for the Archdeaconry Court of London (1700-1807), are online at www.englishorigins.com.

In Scotland testaments of seafarers should be sought amongst the records of the various Commissary (or later the Sheriff's) courts; these are to be found in the main at the National Archives of Scotland. The Scottish Archives Network has published a union index of all Scottish testaments 1513-1901, together with digital copies of the documents, at www.scottishdocuments.com.

The Admiralty seemed to have actively encouraged seamen to make wills and several useful series have survive at TNA, namely:

- *Seamen's Wills, 1786-1882 (ADM 42)* contains original wills of Royal Naval rating and of marines. The series is alphabetically arranged and there is additionally an index in ADM 142.

- *Seamen's Effects Papers, 1800-1860 (ADM 44)* contain claims for back pay of ratings who died in service. Some wills, birth and marriage certificates are included. These are indexed by ADM 141 which has already been described in the section on Admiralty: Deaths in Service, Ratings.

- *Officers and Civilians Effects Papers, 1830-1860 (ADM 45)* is a similar series to that above and has already been described in the section on Admiralty: Deaths in Service, Ratings, Officers and Civilians.

The National Maritime Museum holds some records of the Inspector of Seamen's Wills for the period 1910-1958. These include officers, ratings and civilians giving date and place of birth as well as death. These may duplicate material at TNA in PRO series ADM 242 and ADM 104.

## Census

The various population censuses should not be ignored as an indication of a birth at sea and an age that may be used to calculate a corresponding date. Indeed the ongoing process of creating computer-searchable union indexes to these has opened up the possibility of extracting lists of those who claimed to be born at sea – and there are very significant numbers of them.

## Newspapers

Newspapers may yield the first clue to tracing an event at sea; this could be in the form of an obituary or birth announcement. In addition they may provide much fuller details of the circumstances surrounding an individual death at sea or a marine disaster resulting in considerable loss of life.

If an ancestor was involved in a disaster at sea, then the information obtainable from newspapers can be extensive even if tragic, as the following example, from the *Goole Times* of Friday, August 24th, 1894, illustrates:

# FEARFUL DISASTER IN THE OUSE.

## TWO MEN DROWNED

### A Steamship on Fire

On Monday evening, shortly after half-past eight, the s.s. J.M. Lennard of Middlesbrough, owned by Messrs. Lennard and Sons, of that port, left Goole for Jersey with a cargo of 500 tons of coal. The command of the vessel was entrusted to Captain P. Horne, who had the assistance of Captain Cook, of Hull, as the pilot. She was drawing 15 feet 6 inches of water as she steamed away, and it was noticed that she had some difficulty in stemming the strong tide that was running. Shortly after passing Bennett's Jetty the steering gear failed to operate properly, and the stern of the ship is reported to have caught the sand bank which has recently formed in close proximity to the right bank training wall. Directly this mishap occurred the force of the tide drove the fore part of the vessel with great violence on to the stone wall, and immediately after she was struck she heeled over and became almost submerged in the water. The sudden lurch of the vessel was such that one of the crew was thrown overboard, and he swam ashore. The other members of the crew, including the captain and pilot, were in great peril, for after clinging to the side of the ship, they were conveyed to the shore by boats. When the steamer heaved over on the starboard side, water rushed into the engine room, and in doing so the iron ladders were disarranged, which caused the means of escape less easy. The chief engineer had a desperate struggle for life. Owing to the ladder getting out of position he was thrown back two or three times, but eventually he succeeded in reaching the deck, to find that the readiest means had to be adopted for securing a footing on land. The second engineer, named Cater, and an elderly man Mulholland, a fireman, were not so fortunate, because the inrush of water and the derangement of the means of exit prevented them from reaching the deck, and consequently they were ingulfed in the water that flooded the machine-room. They were heard to cry for help but under the circumstances assistance could not be rendered. It is stated by those who were adjacent that one of the men was heard to hammer at the interior of the ship as a sign that he was alive and required relief, but this signal could not effectually be obeyed. The ingress of water at length filled the engine room and the two men were drowned.

...

Mulholland, who is an aged man, belonged to Goole, but for several years has been engaged in the colliery district, chiefly at Normanton. The man Cater belongs London, and he leaves a widow and two children to mourn his loss.

...

Several efforts have been made to rescue the body of Albert Cater, the second engineer, but up to the present success has not crowned the labours of the police and others who were engaged.

Information about shipwrecks and other marine disasters will be found in both the printed records (*Lloyd's List*) and manuscripts of Lloyds of London[100] and of the Board of Trade.[101]

Newspapers published in the colonies would often contain information about arriving ships. In New Zealand, it would seem,[102] they often included the surgeon's report on passengers' wellbeing and on any births and deaths that had occurred on the voyage.

Newspapers should be sought at the British Library Newspaper Library (Colindale), local Reference Libraries or exceptionally at the office of the newspaper itself.[103] The catalogue of the British Library Newspaper Library (Colindale) is available on-line at http://prodigi.bl.uk/nlcat/.

Not many indexes have been produced to newspapers and those that have are mostly concerned with matter of substance and not with birth announcements and the like. There is a personal name card index to the *Cumberland Pacquet*, at the Whitehaven branch of the Cumbria Record Office, which includes references to many deaths of mariners from the nearby ports of Whitehaven, Maryport, Workington and Harrington.

It is always worth checking the web as you may be lucky and find something like 'San Francisco Genealogy, Vital Notices 1853, Deaths (Deaths aboard ships or at sea and Deaths aboard ships coming to San Francisco)' at http://www.sfgenealogy.com/sf/sf1853d.htm – these are taken from *Daily Alta California* newspapers.

One notable project underway is indexing a number of local Australian newspapers for the second half of the 19th century and is concerned with 'references to any passengers who were on shipping vessels and/or were drowned/lost/survivors at sea'. The GENSEEK 'People at Sea' index is available at www.standard.net.au/ ~jwilliams/people.htm.

## Other official records

The above list cannot in any way be considered comprehensive. For example the records of the High Court of Admiralty, preserved at TNA, will undoubtedly contain information concerning disasters at sea which resulted in loss of life. Searching of these records though is not for the faint-hearted – *see* one of the two standard works on the subject[104] for more details.

The various series of State Papers, preserved at TNA, do undoubtedly contain information about events at sea and this could provide an essential clue. Some of the printed calendars do include lists of names and of ships.

# SEARCH STRATEGIES

## Introduction

In this chapter we will consider how best to use the vast array of available records to trace a birth, death or marriage that took place at sea. The objective will be to track down the primary record source as this should be the most accurate and hopefully the most detailed record of the event – in most cases this will be the ship's log book. But it is most unlikely that you will be able to turn to this source directly and you will need to use a range of secondary and/or subsidiary sources to assist.

In the next section we will guide you through searching for events that were covered by the laws of the United Kingdom. In the final section we will look rather wider to give advice where these initial searches have failed to reveal any record.

## Events covered by UK law

### Births and Deaths

In this section we will look at the steps necessary to trace an event at sea that was registered under the laws of the United Kingdom. This should, in broad terms, cover:

- births and deaths of persons aboard ships registered in Britain and its colonies;

- births and deaths aboard non-British passenger ships arriving at, or departing from UK ports;

but there will be minor variations to this, some of which are date-dependent – this has been explained in earlier chapters.

Finding the primary source, normally the log book as it is the most reliable, accurate and probably the most detailed, is the objective. But the primary sources are not easy to find your way about so we will need to start with the better indexed and more readily accessible subsidiary and secondary sources.

## Step 1 – any subsidiary sources

Check any readily available subsidiary sources, such as those described in the previous chapter, to obtain information about:

The person:

- name of child or deceased
- nationality of parents or deceased
- country of normal residence of parents or deceased

The voyage:

- port of departure
- next port of call after the event
- port of destination

Date of the event:

- to within a few years

The ship:

- Royal Navy, merchant ship, passenger ship
- name of ship and, for merchant vessels, port of registry or Official Number
- country of registration

It is unlikely that you will know, or find, all this information at this stage but whatever you do may help – and you can always come back to try and find more as your search progresses.

If you know the date and the name of the ship on which the event occurred then you may be able to go directly to checking out the primary sources described in Step 4, otherwise proceed to Step 2.

## Step 2 – civil registration

You should now turn your attention to the records of civil registration. If the event that you are trying to trace predates civil registration then you will need to go to Step 3 or more likely Step 4.

Where you need to look will depend on the nationality, or country of normal residence, of the parents of the child or of the deceased (but it may be prudent to check those for England and Wales in addition):

## England & Wales

| Indexes to: | Date | Reason |
|---|---|---|
| Marine Registers of Births and Deaths (including the informal ones) | 1 July 1837 to 1965 | |
| General series births and deaths | 1 July 1837 to date | The event may have taken place in territorial waters |
| Consular Registers | 1849-1965 | The event may have been reported to the British consul or High Commissioner at the ship's next port of call or destination |
| UK High Commission Registers | Births: 1950-1965 Deaths: 1940-1981 | |
| Service Registers (several series – *see* page 98-99) | 1881-1965 | For those who were in the armed services |
| Registers of Births and Deaths Abroad | 1966 to date | These continue all the above series related to events outside the UK |
| Miscellaneous registers transferred to TNA (several series – *see* page 96) | 1831-1931 | |

## Scotland

| Indexes to: | Date | Reason |
|---|---|---|
| Marine Registers of Births and Deaths (including Intimations and not-registered volumes) | 1855 to date | |
| General series births and deaths | 1855 to date | The event may have taken place in territorial waters |
| Consular Registers | 1914 to date | |

| Indexes to: | Date | Reason |
|---|---|---|
| UK High Commissioners' returns of death | 1964 to date | The event may have been reported to the British consul or High Commissioner at the ship's next port of call or destination |
| Returns of births, deaths and marriages in foreign countries | 1860-1965 | |
| Service Registers (several series – *see* page 105) | 1881-1965 | For those who were in the armed services. *Note:* It may also be prudent to look at the equivalent registers held by the GRO (England and Wales) |
| Miscellaneous registers transferred to TNA (several series – *see* page 96) | 1831-1931 | |
| Consular and High Commission Registers at GRO (England and Wales) – *see* above. | 1849 to start of Scottish equivalent | Event may have been recorded here prior to commencement of the equivalent Scottish registers |

## *Ireland - Dublin*

The records at Dublin relate to the whole of Ireland up to 31 December 1921 and thereafter only to the Republic of Ireland. These should apply to events on both British and Irish-registered ships from 1922.

| Indexes to: | Date | Reason |
|---|---|---|
| Marine Registers of Births and Deaths | 1 January 1864 to date | *Note:* Where it was unclear as to whether the residence of the deceased, or the child's parent, was in Northern Ireland or the Republic then the event should be recorded by both GROs |
| General series births and deaths | 1 January 1864 to date | The event may have taken place in territorial waters |
| Consular Registers | 1 January 1864 to 31 December 1921 | The event may have been reported to the British consul at the ship's next port of call or destination |

| Indexes to: | Date | Reason |
|---|---|---|
| Service Registers (several series – *see* page 109-110) | 1881-1965 | For those who were in the armed services.<br>*Note:* It may also be prudent to look at the equivalent registers held by the GRO (England and Wales) |
| Miscellaneous registers transferred to TNA (several series – *see* page 96) | 1831-1931 | |
| Consular and High Commission Registers at GRO (England and Wales) – *see* above. | 1849 to start of Irish equivalent | Event may have been recorded here prior to commencement of the equivalent Irish registers |

## *Northern Ireland – Belfast*

The records at Belfast relate to Northern Ireland from 1 January 1922; they do also have copies of some of the records held in Dublin.

| Indexes to: | Date | Reason |
|---|---|---|
| Marine Registers of Births and Deaths | 1 January 1922 to date | *Note:* Where it was unclear as to whether the residence of the deceased, or the child's parent, was in Northern Ireland or the Republic then the event should be recorded by both GROs |
| General series births and deaths | 1 January 1922 to date | The event may have taken place in territorial waters |
| Consular Registers | 1 January 1922 to date | The event may have been reported to the British consul or High Commissioner at the ship's next port of call or destination |
| UK High Commissioners' returns of births and deaths | 1 January 1950 to date | |

| Indexes to: | Date | Reason |
|---|---|---|
| Service Registers (several series – *see* page 111) | 1881-1965 | For those who were in the armed services. *Note:* It may also be prudent to look at the equivalent registers held by the GRO (England and Wales) |
| Miscellaneous registers transferred to TNA (several series – *see* page 96) | 1831-1931 | |
| Consular and High Commission Registers at GRO (England and Wales) – *see* above. | 1849 to start of Northern Ireland equivalent | Event may have been recorded here prior to commencement of the equivalent Northern Ireland registers |

## *Foreigners*

In general terms registration of births and deaths of foreign nationals, on board ship, were subject to UK law:

• on British-registered ships

• on foreign-registered passenger ships with a port of departure or destination within the UK

• on board ships in territorial waters

but there will be minor variations to this, some of which are date-dependent – this has been explained in earlier chapters. In the last case they would have been reported to the local registrar; in the other two cases they were to be reported to the GRO for England and Wales.

| Indexes to: | Start date | Reason |
|---|---|---|
| Marine Registers of Births and Deaths at GRO (England & Wales) | 1855 | On ships carrying passengers to ports outside Europe or the Mediterranean |
| | 1875 | As above plus all categories of British ships |

| Indexes to: | Start date | Reason |
|---|---|---|
| General series births and deaths at GRO for: | | |
| England & Wales | 1 July 1837 | The event may have taken place in territorial waters |
| Scotland | 1 January 1855 | |
| Ireland | 1 January 1864 | |
| Northern Ireland | 1 January 1922 | |

## *Step 3 – secondary ship records*

Hopefully a search of the civil registration indexes will have revealed the event that you are seeking and allow you to progress to Steps 3 and 4. But if you have not found it then all is not lost since the GRO registers do not cover everything by a very long way.

If you did find an entry then it is not always necessary to purchase a certificate since the various registers and records that you are now going to examine could well duplicate the information. But there are so many exceptions to this that we are reluctant to give this as absolute positive advice.

You should now, hopefully know:

- the nationality of the individual
- whether the event occurred aboard a Royal Navy or a merchant vessel
- whether the individual was a passenger or a crew member
- whether the individual was a serviceman

## *Merchant vessels*

If the event took place on a merchant vessel you should now search the various registers compiled by the Registrar-General of Shipping and Seamen. These have been listed, in detail, by category and year in Appendix 2, Tables 4, 5 and 7. Most series have indexes but some will need to be ordered up individually, year by year, hence the reason for narrowing the search by using the GRO indexes first. You will find that these registers cover:

| Category | Births | Deaths |
|---|---|---|
| Seamen | | 1852-1893 |
| Passengers | 1854-1890 | 1854-1890 |
| 'British Nationals' categorised as which GRO received details:<br>• Scotland – for Scottish subjects<br>• Ireland – for Irish subjects<br>• England – for all others incl. Foreign nationals | 1875-1891 | 1875-1888 |
| General series | 1891-1964 | 1891-1964<br>Separate registers for Seamen and Passengers but with a combined index. |

## Royal Navy ships

If the event took place on a Royal Navy ship you should now search the various registers compiled by the Admiralty. These relate mainly, but not exclusively, to service personnel (Royal Navy and Royal Marines) and do not differentiate between those dying at sea and those ashore. There are few registers related to civilians killed on board naval vessels and none related to births at sea.

The registers that you will need to consider searching are:

- Deaths in service (1802-1878)
  - Dead men's wages (1787-1809)
  - Ratings (1802-1878)
  - Officers and Civilians (1830-1860)

- World War 1
  - Officers
  - Ratings
- Medical Department Registers (1854 onwards)
  - Killed or wounded in action (1854-1929)
  - Deaths other than by enemy action (1893-1956)
  - Deaths by enemy action (July 1900-Oct 1941)
  - Deaths: ratings, World War 2 (1939-1948)

All these are described in the Admiralty chapter.

## *Step 4 – primary sources*

Now you have reached the stage to check the primary sources. If the steps described above have been successful and revealed a ship's name and a date then this process should be straight-forward – if not then you have only guesswork to guide you and thus a lengthy search ahead of you.

## *Merchant ships*

### Log books, crew lists and muster rolls

The primary sources that you should turn to first are the log books, crew lists and muster rolls, but these do not survive for all periods and may be missing if the ship was lost.

- before 1747
  Survival of any log book will be by chance and they could be in any archive.
- 1747-1834
  Survival of any log book will be by chance and they could be in any archive. Muster rolls for a number of ports survive and are to be found at TNA, but these are only likely to mention crew members.

- 1835-1860

  Most crew lists survive and do mention events related to passengers as well as crew. Official log books start in October 1850 but not all have been preserved; those containing details of births, deaths and marriages are more likely to have survived. These records are at TNA. Unofficial log books may have survived by chance and could be in any archive.

- 1861-1938

  All crew lists and official log books should have been preserved but only 10% are at TNA. Details of where to find them are given in Appendix 1.

- 1939-1950

  All crew lists and official log books should have been preserved at TNA.

- 1951-1977

  All crew lists and official log books should have been preserved but only 10% are at TNA. Details of where to find them are given in Appendix 1.

- 1977-1994

  Only 10% of the crew lists and official log books have been preserved; these are at TNA. Those for ships that were involved in the Falklands conflict have all been preserved and are currently with the RSS but will come to TNA in due course.

- 1995 onwards

  Crew lists and official log books for this period are still with the RSS.

## Passenger lists

Passenger lists for vessels arriving at UK ports from places outside Europe or the Mediterranean have survived for the periods 1878-1888 and 1890-1960. These should list events on board involving any passenger wherever embarked. These records are at TNA.

## Other records

There is a range of other primary source material, such as Inquiry reports, B&D1 lists etc, described in the chapter on Merchant Ships and this may usefully be followed up depending on the precise nature of the research.

## Royal Navy ships

### Log books

The primary source for events on Royal Navy ships is the log books. These survive at TNA for the period 1669-1969 with additional lieutenants' logs being found at the NMM.

If no log book can be found then the various series of muster books and pay lists, persevered at TNA, may need to be consulted for deaths of Royal Navy personnel.

### Chaplains records

The records of baptisms and burials performed by chaplains on board RN ships might also be consulted. The returns that went to the Bishop of London's registry are now at the Guildhall Library; those performed by RN chaplains are at TNA.

### *Marriages*

Tracing a marriage on board a British vessel is rather more straight-forward than tracing a birth or death. The method depends on whether the event took place on a merchant ship or a Royal Naval vessel.

### *Merchant ship*

There are two registers of marriage ceremonies performed aboard British vessels, covering the periods 1858-1883 (BT 158/2-4) and 1854-1972 (BT 334/117). Both are indexed and are preserved at TNA. A transcript of these has been compiled by Debbie Beavis and is available on the internet at www.theshipslist.com/Forms/marriagesatsea.html.

It is possible that *Foreign Marriages, 1826-1921 (RG 34)* may contain some entries related to marriages at sea.

Having found the name of the ship on board which the marriage took place and the date, you should now turn to the log book for fuller detail. Details of where to find merchant ship log books are given above (Step 4 on tracing births and deaths on merchant ships – *see* page 142). Most of the log books recording marriages have been preserved at TNA in PRO series BT 165. BT 165/2035 is particularly strong in logs containing marriages and the box contains a list where somebody, probably in 1978, has been attempting to bring this information together for the period 1857-1864.

## Royal Navy ships

Returns of marriages performed on RN vessels from 1842 to 1889 are to be found at TNA in PRO RG 33/156. There is an integral index, and entries are also indexed in RG 43/7. At the Guildhall Library there is also a list of certificates of marriage on board HM ships (1843-1879); these records should correspond to returns just described.

From 1890 one would expect to find any such marriages to be recorded in the *Consular Registers of Marriage, 1849-1965* and subsequently in the *Register of Marriages Abroad* at the GRO for England and Wales. The equivalent consular marriage registers held at the GROs for Scotland (from 1917) and Ireland (Dublin and Belfast) may also contain entries related to persons from those countries.

Marriages of service personnel abroad on board ship may possibly be recorded in the several series of service register, dating from 1881, held by the various GROs. These should be consulted if appropriate.

It is possible that *Foreign Marriages, 1826-1921 (RG 34)* may contain some entries related to marriages at sea.

Having found the name of the ship on board which the marriage took place and the date, you should now turn to the log book. Details of where to find Royal Navy ship log books are given above (Step 4 on tracing births and deaths on Royal Navy ships – *see* page 142).

### Still can't find them?

If after following the suggestions above, and checking all the appropriate sources described elsewhere in this book, you still cannot find a record of the event in question then where might you look?

So far we have been concerned with the records created to meet the requirements of UK law, now we need to look rather wider – and this will certainly apply when searching for information about any persons, including Britons, working or travelling on a foreign vessel. In the paragraphs that follow we pose some questions to guide your future searching. If exploration of these avenues fails, then you may have to face the fact that no record of the event was made or survives... or the event did not actually take place!

*Births and Deaths*

Consider the person's nationality

- Consult the civil registration records for the country of which the deceased, or the child's parents, were nationals; they may have marine or consular registers or other arrangements for the registration of births and deaths of their nationals overseas.

Consider the ship's nation of registration:

- Check for a log book[*], or passenger list, for the ship in the archives of the nation where the ship was registered. These will probably be arranged by date, perhaps under either the final port for the voyage or the port of registry of the ship; alternatively they may be arranged by some official number for the ship.
- Consult the civil registration records for the country in which the ship was registered; they may have required registration of births and deaths on their ships.

Consider the ship's port of departure

- Consult the civil registration records of the country of departure as they may have required registration of events occurring on ships on voyages departing from their country.

Consider the first port of call after the event occurred:

- Births and deaths will most likely have been registered at the next port of call for the ship, so:

---

[*] Wherever it is suggested that a search should be made for a log book do not overlook the possibility that the crew list may have been used for the same purpose even if the parties were passengers.

- check the records of the civil registration authority for that port, state or country<sup>*</sup>.
- if the deceased, or the child's parents, were aliens in that country, then check the records of their nation's consul in that port (these should be in the home country).

- Check for any arriving passenger lists.
- Consult the civil registration records of the country of arrival as they may have required registration of events occurring on ships travelling to their country.

## Consider the ship's port of final destination

- Consult the civil registration records of the country of arrival as they may have required registration of events occurring on ships travelling to their country.
- Check for a log book for the ship.
- Check for any arriving passenger lists.

*Marriages*

- Consult the records of the registration authorities in the state or country of the next port of call for the ship.
- Consult any registers compiled by the minister who conducted the marriage ceremony.
- Consult the records of the ecclesiastic authorities of the church to which the minister, who conducted the marriage ceremony, belonged.
- Consult the consular records of country of which the parties were nationals.
- Check for a log book, or passenger list, for the ship in the archives of the nation in which the ship was registered. These will probably be arranged by date,

---

<sup>*</sup> For example the General Laws of Massachusetts, Chapter 46 Section 7, require that "The master or other commanding officer of a vessel shall give notice, with the facts required for record, of every birth or death occurring among the persons under his charge. The notice of a birth shall be given to the clerk, and the notice of a death shall be given to the board of health or, if the selectmen constitute such board, to the clerk of the town at which his vessel first arrives after such birth or death."

perhaps under either the final port for the voyage or the port of registry of the ship; alternatively the may be arranged by some official number for the ship.

- Consult the civil registration records of the country of arrival (and possibly departure) as they may have required registration of events occurring on ships travelling to or from their country.

# APPENDIX 1
## LOCATION OF AGREEMENTS, CREW LISTS AND LOG BOOKS

**Table 2: Location of Agreements, Crew Lists and Log books**

| Period | Location | Arrangement[*] |
|---|---|---|
| 1835-1844 | TNA: PRO BT 98 | Port of registry, then by ships' names |
| 1845-1856 | TNA: PRO BT 98 | Year, port of registry then by ships' names |
| After 1857 the records are arranged by year, then by ships' official number | | |
| 1857-1860 | TNA: PRO BT 98 and BT 165 | |
| 1861-1912 | • 10% at TNA: PRO BT 99, BT 100, BT 144 and BT 165<br>• Remainder for 1861, 1862, 1865, 1875, 1885, 1895 and 1905 at NMM.<br>• 90% for other years at County Record Offices – *see* Table 3.<br>• Remainder at MHA. | |
| 1913-1938 | • 10% at TNA: PRO BT 99, BT 100, BT 144 and BT 165<br>• Remainder for 1915, 1925 and 1935 at NMM.<br>• 90% for 1913-1921 at National Archives, Dublin – *see* Table 3.<br>• Remainder at MHA; a separate series at the MHA contains Agreements (T124) for vessels hired by the Admiralty for the period of World War 1 (1914-1920) | |
| 1939-1950 | • TNA: PRO BT 99, BT 380, BT 381, and BT 387 | |
| 1951-1976 | • 10% at TNA: PRO BT 99, BT 100 and BT 165<br>• Remainder for 1955, 1965 and 1975 at NMM.<br>• Remainder at MHA. | |
| 1976-1994 | • 10% at TNA: PRO BT 99 and BT 100<br>• Remainder for 1985 at NMM<br>• Vessels involved in the Falklands War are with the RSS<br>• Remainder for other years have been destroyed | |
| 1995 onwards | • RSS | |

---

\* The records of some special categories of vessel may be arranged differently

The above table, although complex, is actually a simplified summary of the situation aimed at directing the researcher to the correct archive. For fuller details and information about finding aids, consult one of the standard works.[105]

**Table 3: County Record Offices holding Crew Lists up to 1912 for ships with Ports of Registry within their area.**

| Record Office or Library[106] | | Ports of Registry/Dates held | |
|---|---|---|---|
| Anglesey CRO | ✓ | Beaumaris (1863-1913) | |
| Berwick-upon-Tweed RO | (✓) | Berwick (1863-1913) | * |
| Bristol RO | ✓ | Bristol (1863-1913) | * |
| Cambridgeshire CRO | ✓ | Wisbech (1863-1913) | |
| Carmarthenshire RO | | Carmarthen, Llanelly (1863-1913) | |
| Centre for Kentish Studies, Maidstone | ✓ | Faversham (1863-1913) | |
| Ceredigion Archives | | Aberystwyth (1863-1913) (small sample) | * |
| Cheshire RO | ✓ | Runcorn (1863-1913) | |
| Cornwall RO | ✓ | Falmouth, Fowey, Padstow, Penzance, St Ives, Truro (1863-1913) | |
| Cumbria RO, Barrow in Furness | ✓ | Barrow (1863-1913) | |
| Cumbria RO, Carlisle | ✓ | Carlisle, Maryport (1863-1913) | |
| Cumbria RO, Whitehaven | ✓ | Whitehaven (1863-1914), Maryport (1863-1911) | |
| Devon RO | ✓ | Barnstaple, Bideford, Dartmouth, Exeter, Ilfracombe, Plymouth, Teignmouth (1863-1913) | * |
| Dorset RO | ✓ | Bridport (1863-1901), Lyme Regis (1863-1912), Poole, Weymouth, (1863-1913) | * |
| East Kent Archive Centre | (✓) | Deal (1863-1874), Dover (1863-1913), Folkestone (1880-1897), Ramsgate (1863-1913) | * |
| Essex RO | ✓ | Harwich, Colchester, Maldon (1863-1913) | |
| Flintshire RO | (✓) | Chester (1863-1913) [records originally at Chester County Archives] plus some misc. | * |
| Glamorgan RO | ✓ | Cardiff (1863-1913) | |
| Glasgow City RO | | ports in Scotland [Later transferred to Newfoundland] | |
| Gloucester CRO | ✓ | Gloucester (1863-1913) | |
| Gwent RO | ✓ | Chepstow, Newport (1869, 1879, 1889, 1899, 1909) | * |
| Gwynedd, Caernarfon area RO | | Caernarvon (1863-1913) | |
| Gwynedd, Dolgellau area RO | ✓ | Aberdovey ships (registered Aberystwyth) (1863-1913) | |

| Record Office or Library[106] | Ports of Registry/Dates held | |
|---|---|---|
| Hull City Archives | Hull fishing vessels (1884-1913) | |
| Lancashire RO ✓ | Fleetwood, Lancaster, Preston (1863-1913) | |
| Lincolnshire Archives | Boston (1863-1913), Gainsborough (1862-1881) | |
| Liverpool RO ✓ | Liverpool (1863-1913) | * |
| Manchester Local Studies Unit Archives ✓ | Manchester (1894-1913) | |
| Manx National Heritage Library | Castletown, Douglas, Peel, Ramsey (1863-1913) | * |
| Rochester upon Medway Studies Centre | Rochester | |
| Merseyside Maritime Museum | Misc. small sample (1863-1913) | * |
| National Archives of Ireland, Dublin ✓ | Ports now in Eire (1863-1921) | μ |
| National Archives of Scotland | Scottish ships (1867-1913) | |
| National Library of Australia | Voyages to Australia and New Zealand (only 81 ships, 1861-1900) | |
| National Library of Wales ✓ | Aberystwyth (1863-1913) | * |
| NE Lincolnshire Archives, Grimsby | Grimsby (1863-1914) | * |
| Norfolk RO | Great Yarmouth, 1863-1913 [Later transferred to Newfoundland] | |
| North Yorkshire CRO | Middlesbrough, Whitby, Scarborough (1861-1867, 1872). | μ |
| Northumberland RO ✓ | Blyth (1863-1913) | |
| Pembrokeshire RO ✓ | Cardigan, Milford Haven (1863-1913) | * |
| Portsmouth City Museums and Records Service ✓ | Portsmouth, Cowes (1863-1913) | * |
| Public Record Office of Northern Ireland ✓ | Ports in Northern Ireland (1857-1938): Belfast, Coleraine, Londonderry, Newry, Strangford | μ |
| Somerset Archives and Record Service ✓ | Bridgwater (1863-1913) | * |
| Southampton Archives Service ✓ | Southampton (1863-1913) | * |
| Suffolk RO, Ipswich ✓ | Ipswich, Woodbridge (1863-1913) | * |
| Suffolk RO, Lowestoft | Lowestoft (1863-1913) | * |
| Tyne & Wear Archives Service ✓ | Shields (1863-1913) [formerly at Northumberland RO] | * |
| West Glamorgan Archives Service, Swansea ✓ | Swansea (1863-1913) | * |
| West Sussex RO ✓ | Arundel, Chichester, Littlehampton, Shoreham (1863-1913) | * |

A ✓ indicates that the holdings of those record offices or libraries have been included in *A Guide to the Crew Agreements and Official Logbooks, 1863-1913, held at the County Record Offices of the British Isles* published by the Maritime History Archive, Memorial University of Newfoundland; but a significant number of transfers between record offices have taken place since that publication was compiled.

A μ indicates that the collection has been filmed. Those for Ireland are available through LDS Family History Libraries; copies of those at Northallerton are available at the Teeside Archives Service in Middlesbrough.

An * indicates that some indexing of names has taken place – enquire at the relevant archives in the first instance.

Where ships were registered in the colonies and operated solely in colonial waters it seems unlikely that their crew lists were ever returned to the UK and these should be sought in the appropriate national or state archives.

# APPENDIX 2
## REGISTERS OF BIRTHS, DEATHS AND MARRIAGES
## COMPILED BY THE RGSS

## Table 4: Births (1854-1891)

| | Passengers | | All British-registered ships and foreign-registered passenger ships to/from UK[*] | | |
| | Indexed registers | Index | English, Welsh, & Foreign | Scottish subjects | Irish subjects |
|---|---|---|---|---|---|
| Series ▶ | BT 158 | BT 158 | BT 160 | BT 160 | BT 160 |
| Year Piece ▼ ▶ | | | | | |
| 1854 | 1 | | | | |
| 1855 | 1 | | | | |
| 1856 | 1 | | | | |
| 1857 | 1 | | | | |
| 1858 | 1 and 2 | | | | |
| 1859 | 2 | | | | |
| 1860 | 2 | | | | |
| 1861 | 2 | | | | |
| 1862 | 2 | | | | |
| 1863 | 2 | | | | |
| 1864 | 2 | | | | |
| 1865 | 2 and 3 | | | | |
| 1866 | 3 | | | | |
| 1867 | 3 | | | | |
| 1868 | 3 | | | | |
| 1869 | 3 | | | | |
| 1870 | 3 | | | | |
| 1871 | 3 | | | | |
| 1872 | 4 | 7 | | | |
| 1873 | 4 | 7 | | | |
| 1874 | 4 | 7 | | | |
| 1875 | 4 | 7 | 1 | 5 | 3 |
| 1876 | 4 | 7 | 1 | 5 | 3 |
| 1877 | 4 | 7 | 1 | 5 | 3 |
| 1878 | 4 | 7 | 1 | 5 | 3 |
| 1879 | 4 | 7 | 1 | 5 | 3 |
| 1880 | 4 | 7 | 1 | 5 | 3 |
| 1881 | 4 | 7 | 1 | 5 | 3 |

[*] There is little evidence that these registers actually contain a record of events on foreign-registered passenger ships to/from the UK as they should.

| | Passengers | | All British-registered ships and foreign-registered passenger ships to/from UK* | | |
|---|---|---|---|---|---|
| | Indexed registers | Index | English, Welsh, & Foreign | Scottish subjects | Irish subjects |
| Series ► | BT 158 | BT 158 | BT 160 | BT 160 | BT 160 |
| Year Piece ▼ ► | | | | | |
| 1882 | 4 | 7 | 1 | 5 | 3 |
| 1883 | 4 and 5 | 7 | 1 | 5 | 3 |
| 1884 | 5 | 7 | 1 | 5 | 3 |
| 1885 | 5 | 7 and 9 | 2 | 5 | 3 |
| 1886 | 5 | 7 and 9 | 2 | 6 | 4 |
| 1887 | 5 | 7 and 9 | 2 | 6 | 4 |
| 1888 | 9 | 7 and 9 | 2 | 6 | 4 |
| 1889 | 9 | 8 | 2 | 6 | 4 |
| 1890 | | 8 | 2 | 6 | 4 |
| 1891 | | | 2 | 6 | 4 |

For later registers and indexes, *see* series BT 334 (Table 7)

### Table 5: Deaths (1852-1893)

| | Wages & Effects of deceased seamen | | | Deaths of Seamen | | Deaths of Passengers | | Deaths on all British-registered ships and foreign-registered passenger ships to/from UK* | | |
|---|---|---|---|---|---|---|---|---|---|---|
| | Registers | Index to names | Index to ships | by date | by cause | Indexed registers | Index | English, Welsh, Foreign | Scottish subjects | Irish subjects |
| Series ► | BT 153 | BT 154 | BT 155 | BT 156 | BT 157 | BT 158 | BT 158 | BT 159 | BT 159 | BT 159 |
| Year Piece ▼ ► | | | | | | | | | | |
| 1852 | 1 | | | | | | | | | |
| 1853 | 1 | 1 | | | | | | | | |
| 1854 | 1 | 1 | | | | 1 | | | | |
| 1855 | 2 | 2 | 1 | | | 1 | | | | |
| 1856 | 2 | 2 | 1 | | | 1 | | | | |
| 1857 | 2 & 3 | 2 & 3 | 1 | | | 1 | | | | |
| 1858 | 3 | 3 | 1 & 2 | | | 1 & 2 | | | | |
| 1859 | 3 & 4 | 3 | 2 | | | 2 | | | | |
| 1860 | 4 | 4 | 2 | | | 2 | | | | |
| 1861 | 4 | 4 | 2 | | | 2 | | | | |
| 1862 | 4 & 5 | 4 | 2 | | | 2 | | | | |

* There is little evidence that these registers actually contain a record of events on foreign-registered passenger ships to/from the UK as they should.

| | Wages & Effects of deceased seamen | | | Deaths of Seamen | | Deaths of Passengers | | Deaths on all British-registered ships and foreign-registered passenger ships to/from UK[*] | | |
|---|---|---|---|---|---|---|---|---|---|---|
| | Registers | Index to names | Index to ships | by date | by cause | Indexed registers | Index | English, Welsh, Foreign | Scottish subjects | Irish subjects |
| Series ▶ | BT 153 | BT 154 | BT 155 | BT 156 | BT 157 | BT 158 | BT 158 | BT 159 | BT 159 | BT 159 |
| Year Piece ▼ ▶ | | | | | | | | | | |
| 1863 | 5 | 4 | 2 & 3 | | | 2 | | | | |
| 1864 | 5 | 5 | 3 | | | 2 | | | | |
| 1865 | 5 | 5 | 3 | | | 2 & 3 | | | | |
| 1866 | 5 & 6 | 5 & 6 | 3 | | | 3 | | | | |
| 1867 | 7 | 6 | 3 | | | 3 | | | | |
| 1868 | 8 | 7 | 4 | | | 3 | | | | |
| 1869 | 9 | 7 | 4 | | | 3 | | | | |
| 1870 | 10 | 7 | 4 | | | 3 | | | | |
| 1871 | 11 | 7 | 5 | | | 3 | | | | |
| 1872 | 12 | 8 | 5 | | | 4 | 7 | | | |
| 1873 | 13 | 8 | 5 | | | 4 | 7 | | | |
| 1874 | 14 | 8 | 6 | | | 4 | 7 | | | |
| 1875 | 15 | 8 | 6 | | | 4 | 7 | 1 | 8 | 6 |
| 1876 | 15 & 16 | 9 | 7 | | | 4 | 7 | 1 | 8 | 6 |
| 1877 | 17 | 9 | 7 | | | 4 | 7 | 1 & 2 | 8 | 6 |
| 1878 | 18 | 9 | 7 | | | 4 | 7 | 2 | 8 | 6 |
| 1879 | 19 | 10 | 8 | | | 4 | 7 | 2 & 3 | 8 & 9 | 6 |
| 1880 | 20 | 10 | 8 | | | 4 | 7 | 3 | 9 | 6 |
| 1881 | 21 & 22 | 10 & 11 | 8 | | | 4 | 7 | 3 | 9 | 7 |
| 1882 | | 11 | 8 | 1 | | 4 | 7 | 4 | 9 | 7 |
| 1883 | | 12 | 9 | | 2 & 3 | 4 & 5 | 7 | 4 | 9 | 7 |
| 1884 | | 12 | 9 | | 4 & 5 | 5 | 7 | 4 | 9 | 7 |
| 1885 | | 12 & 13 | 9 | | 6 & 7 | 5 | 7 & 9 | 4 | 9 | 7 |
| 1886 | | 13 | 9 & 10 | 1 | 8 | 5 | 7 & 9 | 5 | 10 | 7 |
| 1887 | | 14 | 10 | 1 | 8 & 9 | 5 | 7 & 9 | 5 | 10 | 7 |
| 1888 | 21 | 10 & 14 | 10 | 2 | 9 | 6 & 9 | 7 & 9 | 5 | 10 | 7 |
| 1889 | 21 | 14 | 10 | 3 | | 6 & 9 | 8 | | | |
| 1890 | 21 | | | 4 | | 6 | 8 | | | |
| 1891 | 21 | | | | | | | | | |
| 1892 | 21 | For later registers and indexes, *see* series BT 334 (Table 7) | | | | | | | | |
| 1893 | 21 | | | | | | | | | |

---

[*] There is little evidence that these registers actually contain a record of events on foreign-registered passenger ships to/from the UK as they should.

155

# Table 6: Marriages (1858-1883)[*]

| Series ▶ | Passengers - Indexed Registers BT 158 | | Series ▶ | Passengers - Indexed Registers BT 158 | | Series ▶ | Passengers - Indexed Registers BT 158 |
|---|---|---|---|---|---|---|---|
| Year Piece ▼ ▶ | | | Year Piece ▼ ▶ | | | Year Piece ▼ ▶ | |
| 1858 | 2 | | 1870 | 3 | | 1882 | 4 |
| 1859 | 2 | | 1871 | 3 | | 1883 | 4 |
| 1860 | 2 | | 1872 | 4 | | For later registers and indexes, *see* BT 334/117 (Table 7) | |
| 1861 | 2 | | 1873 | 4 | | | |
| 1862 | 2 | | 1874 | 4 | | | |
| 1863 | 2 | | 1875 | 4 | | | |
| 1864 | 2 | | 1876 | 4 | | | |
| 1865 | 2 and 3 | | 1877 | 4 | | | |
| 1866 | 3 | | 1878 | 4 | | | |
| 1867 | 3 | | 1879 | 4 | | | |
| 1868 | 3 | | 1880 | 4 | | | |
| 1869 | 3 | | 1881 | 4 | | | |

* Information in these registers is probably duplicated in BT 334/117

## Table 7: Births (1891-1960), Marriages (1854-1972) and Deaths (1891-1964) at Sea – BT 334

| Date | INDEXES | | REGISTERS | | | | Date |
|------|---------|--------|--------|-------------------|----------------------|---------------------------------------|------|
|      | Births  | Deaths | Births | Deceased Seamen | Deceased Passengers | Others                                |      |
| 1891 | /1      |        | /4     | /3                | /2                   |                                       | 1891 |
| 1892 | /5      |        |        | /6                |                      |                                       | 1892 |
| 1893 | /7      |        |        | /8                |                      |                                       | 1893 |
| 1894 | /9      |        |        | /10               |                      |                                       | 1894 |
| 1895 | /11     |        |        | /12               | /14                  |                                       | 1895 |
| 1896 | /13     |        |        | /15               |                      |                                       | 1896 |
| 1897 | /16     |        |        | /17               |                      |                                       | 1897 |
| 1898 | /18     |        |        | /19               |                      |                                       | 1898 |
| 1899 | /20     |        |        | /21               | /22                  |                                       | 1899 |
| 1900 | /23     |        |        | /24               |                      |                                       | 1900 |
| 1901 | /25     |        |        | /28               |                      |                                       | 1901 |
| 1902 | /26     |        |        | /29               | /27                  |                                       | 1902 |
| 1903 | /30     |        |        | /31               |                      |                                       | 1903 |
| 1904 | /32     |        |        | /33               |                      |                                       | 1904 |
| 1905 | /35     |        | /34    | /36               |                      |                                       | 1905 |
| 1906 | /37     |        |        | /38               | /41                  |                                       | 1906 |
| 1907 | /39     |        |        | /40               |                      |                                       | 1907 |
| 1908 | /42     |        |        | /43               |                      |                                       | 1908 |
| 1909 | /44     |        |        | /45               | /48                  |                                       | 1909 |
| 1910 | /47     |        |        | /46               |                      | Births and Deaths reported to the GROs /54 | 1910 |
| 1911 | /50     |        |        | /49               |                      | Births and Deaths reported to the GROs /55 | 1911 |
| 1912 | /51     |        | /57    | /53               | /52                  | Deaths of Seamen reported to          | 1912 |
| 1913 | /59     |        |        | /58               |                      | the GROs /56                          | 1913 |
| 1914 | /61     |        |        | /62               | /60                  | Deaths of Seamen reported to          | 1914 |
| 1915 | /64     |        |        | /65               |                      | the GROs /63                          | 1915 |
| 1916 | /66     |        |        | /67               | /68                  | Deaths of Seamen reported to          | 1916 |
| 1917 | /70     |        |        | /71               |                      | the GROs /69                          | 1917 |
| 1918 | /72     |        |        | /73               |                      | Deaths of Seamen reported to the GROs /74 | 1918 |
| 1919 | /75     |        |        | /76               | /79                  |                                       | 1919 |
| 1920 | /77     |        | /81    | /80               |                      |                                       | 1920 |

| Date | INDEXES | | REGISTERS | | | Others | Date |
|------|---------|--------|-----------|-----------------|--------------------|--------|------|
| | Births | Deaths | Births | Deceased Seamen | Deceased Passengers | | |
| 1921 | /78 | | /81 | /80 | /79 | | 1921 |
| 1922 | | | | | /82 | | 1922 |
| 1923 | | | | /84 | | | 1923 |
| 1924 | /83 | | | | | | 1924 |
| 1925 | | | | | | | 1925 |
| 1926 | | | | /86 | /85 | | 1926 |
| 1927 | | | | | | | 1927 |
| 1928 | /88 | | | | | | 1928 |
| 1929 | | | | /89 | /87 | | 1929 |
| 1930 | | | | | | | 1930 |
| 1931 | | | | | | | 1931 |
| 1932 | /91 | | | | | | 1932 |
| 1933 | | | /90 | /92 | | | 1933 |
| 1934 | | | | | | | 1934 |
| 1935 | | | | | /94 | | 1935 |
| 1936 | /95 | | | | | | 1936 |
| 1937 | | | | /93 | | | 1937 |
| 1938 | | | | | | | 1938 |
| 1939 | | | | | | | 1939 |
| 1940 | | | | /96 | /100 | | 1940 |
| 1941 | /97 | | | /98 | | | 1941 |
| 1942 | | | | /99 | | | 1942 |
| 1943 | /101 | | | Jan-June /102 July-Dec /103 | | | 1943 |
| 1944 | | | | /104 | | | 1944 |
| 1945 | /105 | | | | | | 1945 |
| 1946 | | | | /106 | /107 | | 1946 |
| 1947 | | | | | | | 1947 |
| 1948 | | | | | | | 1948 |
| 1949 | | | | | | | 1949 |
| 1950 | /108 | /109 | | /110 | | | 1950 |
| 1951 | | | | | | | 1951 |
| 1952 | | | | | | | 1952 |
| 1953 | | | | | | | 1953 |
| 1954 | | /111 | | | | | 1954 |
| 1955 | | | | | | | 1955 |
| 1956 | | | | | | | 1956 |
| 1957 | | | | /112 | /114 | | 1957 |
| 1958 | | | | | | | 1958 |

| Date | INDEXES | | REGISTERS | | | Others | Date |
|------|---------|--------|--------|-------------------|---------------------|--------|------|
|      | Births  | Deaths | Births | Deceased Seamen | Deceased Passengers |        |      |
| 1959 | /108    | /111   | /90    | /112              | /114                |        | 1959 |
| 1960 |         |        |        |                   |                     |        | 1960 |
| 1961 | None    | /115   | None   | /113              | /116                |        | 1961 |
| 1962 |         |        |        |                   |                     |        | 1962 |
| 1963 |         |        |        |                   |                     |        | 1963 |
| 1964 |         |        |        |                   |                     |        | 1964 |

BT 334/117 Register of Marriages at Sea, 1854-1972

# APPENDIX 3
## ABBREVIATIONS USED IN RGSS REGISTERS

**Trade or Destination**

In the records of the RGSS and Lloyds, a number of abbreviations are used to indicate the trade, destination or voyage of a vessel:

| | |
|---|---|
| A | West Coast of Africa and adjacent islands |
| Aust | Australia, Tasmania, New Zealand |
| B | Baltic, Norway, White Sea, Gulf of Finland and Cattegat |
| C | China, Japan and oriental archipelago |
| Cp | Cape colonies, Ascension, St Helena, Natal, Algoa Bay |
| Ct | Coasting trade, including Holland, Belgium, France, from River Elbe to Brest |
| EI | East Indies, Burma, Mauritius, Red Sea |
| Foreign | — |
| FPS | France (South of Brest), Portugal, Spain (outside Straits of Gibraltar), Azores |
| HT | Home Trade |
| M | Mediterranean, Black Sea, Sea of Azoff, Adriatic |
| NA | British North America, Greenland, Iceland |
| NP | North Pacific and West Coast of North America |
| NS | West Coast of Denmark |
| SA | Brazils, River Plate |
| SP | South Pacific and West Coast of South America |
| Trawling | — |
| US | United States (East Coast and Gulf ports) |
| WI | West Indies and Gulf of Mexico |

# APPENDIX 4
## USEFUL ADDRESSES

### UNITED KINGDOM AND IRELAND

**British Library**
www.bl.uk/
- **Newspaper Library**
Colindale Avenue, London NW9 HE.
newspaper@bl.uk
- **Oriental and India Office Collections**
96 Euston Road, London NW1 2DB.
oioc-enquiries@bl.uk

**County Record Offices**
Addresses are to be found in *Record Repositories in Great Britain* (HMSO), *Record Offices: How to find them* (FFHS) or any good genealogical book. Many have websites that may be located using any good search engine.

**Family Records Centre**
1 Myddelton Street, London EC1R 1UW.
www.familyrecords.gov.uk/frc/

**General Register Offices**
- **England and Wales**
*Personal enquiries*
*– see* Family Records Centre
*Postal enquiries:*
Office for National Statistics, Smedley Hydro, Trafalgar Road, Southport, Merseyside, PR8 2HH.
www.statistics.gov/registration
certificate.services@ons.gov.uk

- **Scotland**
General Register Office for Scotland, New Register House, Edinburgh EH1 3YT.
www.gro-scotland.gov.uk
records@gro-scotland.gov.uk
- **Northern Ireland**
General Register Office (Northern Ireland), Oxford House, 49-55 Chichester Street, Belfast BT1 4HL.
www.nics.gov.uk/nisra/gro/
- **Ireland**
General Register Office of Ireland 8-11 Lombard Street East, Dublin 2, Republic of Ireland.
www.groireland.ie/

**Guildhall Library**
Aldermanbury, London EC2P 2EJ.
www.ihrinfo.ac.uk/gh/
manuscripts.guildhall@ms.corpoflond on.gov.uk
printedbooks.guildhall@ms.corpoflon don.gov.uk

**National Archives of Ireland**
Bishop Street, Dublin 8, Republic of Ireland
www.nationalarchives.ie/
mail@nationalarchives.ie

**National Maritime Museum**
Greenwich, London SE10 9NF.
www.nmm.ac.uk
library@nmm.ac.uk
manuscripts@nmm.ac.uk

Research enquires to:
lxveri@nmm.ac.uk

**Registry of Shipping & Seamen**
Marine & Coastguard Agency, Anchor
Court, Keen Road, Cardiff, CF24
5JW.
www.mcagency.org.uk
rss@mcga.gov.uk

**Society of Genealogists**
14 Charterhouse Buildings,
Goswell Road, London EC1M 7BA
www.sog.org.uk
library@sog.org.uk

**The National Archives (Public
Record Office)**
Ruskin Avenue, Kew, Richmond,
Surrey TW9 4DU.
www.nationalarchives.gov.uk
enquiry@nationalarchives.gov.uk

**Whitby Museum**
Pannett Park, Whitby, North Yorkshire
YO21 1RE.
www.durain.demon.co.uk
graham@durain.demon.co.uk
*or* rlp@cwcom.net

## OVERSEAS

**Argentina**
• **Archivo General de la Nación**
Leandro N. Alem 246, C1003AAP
Buenos Aires, Argentina.
www.archivo.gov.ar/
archivo@mininterior.gov.ar

• **Centros de Estudios Migratorios
de Latinoamericos**
CEMLA,
Independencia 20,
(1099) Buenos Aires, Argentina
www.cemla.com/
cemla@ciudad.com.ar

**Australia: State Archives**
• **State Records, New South Wales**
PO Box 516, Kingswood, NSW 2747.
www.records.nsw.gov.au
srecords@records.nsw.gov.au

• **State Records of South Australia**
Basement, State Library Building,
North Terrace, Adelaide,
South Australia.
www.archives.sa.gov.au
staterecords@saugov.sa.gov.au

• **State Records Office of Western
Australia**
Alexander Library Building,
James Street West Entrance,
Perth Cultural Centre, Perth,
Western Australia 6000.
www.sro.wa.gov.au/
sro@sro.wa.gov.au

**Australia:  State Registries (b,d&m)**
Current postal and e-mail addresses
and links to websites are to be found
at: www.bdm.nsw.gov.au/bdmaus/

• **New South Wales**
Principal Registrar,
Births, Deaths & Marriages
PO Box 30, Sydney, NSW 2001.

- **Victoria**
Registrar, Births, Deaths & Marriages
PO Box 4332, Melbourne, Vic 3001.

- **Queensland**
Registrar, Births, Deaths & Marriages
PO Box 188, Albert St, Qld 4002.

- **South Australia**
Registrar, Births, Deaths & Marriages
Registration Office, PO Box 1351,
Adelaide, SA 5001.

- **Western Australia**
Registry of, Births, Deaths &
Marriages, PO Box 7720,
Cloisters Square, WA 6850.

- **Tasmania**
Registry of Births, Deaths &
Marriages, GPO Box 198, Hobart, Tas
7001.

- **Northern Territory**
Registrar General,
Births, Deaths & Marriages
PO Box 3021, Darwin, NT 0801.

- **Australian Capital Territory**
Registrar, Births, Deaths & Marriages
PO Box 225, Civic Square,
ACT 2608.

**Australian National Archives**:
www.naa.gov.au/
archives@naa.gov.au

- **Canberra**
PO Box 8425, Canberra Mail Centre,
ACT 2610.

- **New South Wales Regional Office**
120 Miller Road, Chester Hill,
NSW 2162.

- **Queensland Regional Office**
PO Box 552, Cannon Hill,
Qld 4170.

- **South Australia Regional Office**
PO Box 6356, Adelaide, SA 5000.

**Australia: overseas registrations**
Department of Immigration and
Multicultural Affairs, PO Box 25,
Belconnen, ACT 2616.

**Australian Service Deaths:**

- **Air Force**
Air Force Career Management Branch,
Defence Personnel Executive,
E-2-25, Russell Offices,
Canberra, ACT 2601.

- **Army**
Soldier Career Management Agency
GPO Box 393D, Melbourne,
Vic 3001.

- **Navy**
Directorate of Naval Personnel
Services
D-3-15, Russell Offices,
Canberra, ACT 2601.

**Hudson's Bay Company Archives**
Archives of Manitoba,
200 Vaughan Street, Winnipeg,
Manitoba, Canada R3C 1T5
www.gov.mb.ca/chc/archives/hbca/
hbca@gov.mb.ca

**Maritime History Archive**
Memorial University of
Newfoundland, St. John's,
Newfoundland, Canada A1C 5S7.
www.mun.ca/mha/
mha@mun.ca

**Canada: National Archives**
National Archives of Canada
395 Wellington Street, Ottawa,
Ontario K1A 0N3, Canada.
www.archives.ca/

**New Zealand: National Archives**
Archives New Zealand
PO Box 12-050,
Wellington, New Zealand.
www.archives.govt.nz/
enquiries@archives.govt.nz

**New Zealand: Registry (b,d&m)**
Central Registry,
Births, Deaths & Marriages,
PO Box 10-526
47 Boulcott Street
Wellington, New Zealand.
www.bdm.govt.nz/
bdm.nz@dia.govt.nz

# APPENDIX 5
## BIBLIOGRAPHY AND REFERENCES

*Notes:* References denoted by a symbol (such as $^{*,\dagger,\ddagger,\S}$) are footnotes and are to be found at the bottom of the page on which they appear.

Unless otherwise stated all document referred to are held at The National Archives of the UK.

### Some warnings!

[1]  Colledge, J J, *Ships of the Royal Navy* (Greenhill, 2 vols. 1987-1989) .
Warlow, B, *Shore establishments of the Royal Navy : being a list of the static ships and establishments of the Royal Navy* (Liskeard, Cornwall: Maritime Books, 1992).

### Introduction

[2]  *The British Overseas*, Guildhall Library Research Guide 2 (3rd edn. Guildhall Library, 1994) p.9 *et loc.cit.*
Ridge, A D, 'All at Sea: Observations on the Stepney Baptism Registers', *Archives*, vol.6, no.31 (October 1964) pp.229-234.

[3]  Camp, A J, 'Births, marriages and deaths at sea', *Family Tree Magazine* vol.17 no.2 pp.9-10 (December 2000).

### Legislation and Regulations

[4]  Registration of Births and Deaths Act 1836, 6 & 7 Will IV c.86 s.21.

[5]  Registration of Births and Deaths Act 1836, 6 & 7 Will IV c.86 s.26.

[6]  Registration of Births Deaths and Marriages Act (Scotland) 1854, 17 & 18 Vic c.80 s.30.

[7]  Registration of Births Deaths and Marriages Act (Scotland) 1854, 17 & 18 Vic c.80 s.43.

[8]  Registration of Births and Deaths Act (Ireland) 1863, 26 & 27 Vic c.11 s.39.

[9] Registration of Births, and Deaths Act (Ireland) 1863, 26 & 27 Vic c.11 s.40.

[10] Registration of Births and Deaths Act 1874, 37 & 38 Vic c.88 s.37

[11] Merchant Shipping Act 1894, 57 & 58 Vic c.60 ss.254 and 339.

[12] An Act for the further Support and Encouragement of the Fisheries carried on in the Greenland Seas and Davis's Streights, 26 Geo III c.41 and An Act for the Encouragement of the Southern Whale Fishery, 26 Geo III c.50.

[13] An Act to continue, for a limited Time, and amend an Act, made in the last session of Parliament intituled, *An Act to regulate, for a limited Time, the shipping and carrying of Slaves in British Vessels from the Coast of Africa*, 29 Geo III c.66.

[14] An Act for regulating the Vessels carrying Passengers from the United Kingdom to His Majesty's Plantations and Settlements Abroad or to Foreign Parts with respect to the Number of such Passengers, 43 Geo III c.56.

[15] Mercantile Marine Act, 1850, 13 & 14 Vic c.93 ss.87, 89 and 90.

[16] Merchant Shipping Act 1854, 17 & 18 Vic c.104 s.27.

[17] Merchant Shipping Act 1894, 57 & 58 Vic c.60 ss.239 and 253.

[18] The quoted text comes from a sample on a file dated 1932 (PRO RG 48/1049) but is typical of what is to be found.

[19] This information is extracted from a B&D1 form dated 1945, preserved at the NMM, but is typical of what is to be found.

[20] An Act for the prevention of Desertion of Seaman from British Merchant Ships trading to His Majesty's Colonies and Plantations in the West Indies, 37 Geo III c.73 ss.7-8.

[21] Seamen's Fund Winding-up Act 1851, 14 & 15 Vic c.102 ss.29, 31 and 32.

[22] Merchant Shipping Act 1854, 17 & 18 Vic c.104 s.194.

[23] Merchant Shipping Act 1970, 19 Eliz II c.36 s.72(b).

[24] Passenger Act 1855, 18 & 19 Vic c.119 s.100.

[25] Aliens Act 1905, 5 Edw VII c.13 and Merchant Shipping Act 1906, 6 Edw VII c.48.

[26] Passenger Act 1855, 18 & 19 Vic c.119 s.16.

[27] *King's Regulations and Admiralty Instructions (1906)* Articles 1559 and 1853 (as amended by Circular Letter No. 112, N.P. 2566, 24 December 1909) – copy in PRO ADM 1/8311.

[28] *Queen's Regulations and Admiralty Instructions, 1862* Chapter 35 Article 21 (p 258) and Appendix p.126-7.

[29] *See* PRO BT 167/151 p.79 – extracted from file MC 33/4/001

[30] *Abstract of arrangements respecting registration of births, marriages and deaths in the United Kingdom and other countries of the British Commonwealth of Nations and in the Irish Republic* (HMSO, 1952) p.183.

[31] *King's Regulations and Admiralty Instructions, 1923*, Article 2104 – a copy of this regulation is in PRO RG 48/638. Reference is also made to Article 1571.

[32] Letter dated 23rd March 1922 on PRO RG 48/407.

[33] An Act for the Relief and Support of maimed and disabled seamen and the Widows and Children of such as shall be killed, slain or drowned in the Merchant Service 1746, 20 Geo II c.38 and amending Acts of 1834 (4 & 5 Will IV c.52) and 1844 (7 & 8 Vic c.52).

[34] An Act for the Relief and Support of maimed and disabled seamen and the Widows and Children of such as shall be killed, slain or drowned in the Merchant Service 1746, 20 Geo II c.38, s.20.

[35] An Act to amend (20 Geo II c.38), 4 & 5 Will IV c.52 s.10.

[36] Seamen's Fund Winding-up Act, 14 & 15 Vic c.102.

[37] *King's Regulations and Admiralty Instructions, 1923*, Article 1857 – a copy of this regulation is in PRO RG 48/638.

[38] PRO MT 23/603 file T91990/1916.

[39] Merchant Shipping Act 1854, 17 & 18 Vic c.104 s.448.

[40] For a fuller discussion on this point *see*: Beavis, D, 'Myths of marriage at sea', *Family Tree Magazine*, vol.19, no.2 (December 2002) pp.61-63. But, contrary to the statement therein, the Merchant Shipping Act 1894, 57 & 58 Vic c.60 s.240(6) does not specifically warn the master of a merchant ships that 'any

ceremony performed by him would not be legal'; that point is made by the RGGS in the advice to masters printed in every logbook.

[41] Merchant Shipping Act 1854, 17 & 18 Vic c.104 s.282.

[42] Merchant Shipping Act 1894, 57 & 58 Vic c.60 ss.240(6) and 253(1)(viii).

[43] *See* PRO BT 167/151 M7746/36 and record series PRO RG 48.

[44] PRO RG 48/1049.

[45] PRO RG 48/294.

[46] For a fuller discussion on irregular marriages, *see* Steel, D J, *National Index of Parish Registers, Vol XII: Sources for Scottish Genealogy and Family History*, (Society of Genealogists, 1970), pp.98-109.

[47] May, A S, 'Marriages at Sea', *The Seaman*, Wednesday September 21 1932 p.7 col.3.

[48] For a fuller explanation *see: The British Overseas*, Guildhall Library Research Guide 2 (3rd edn. Guildhall Library, 1994) footnote on p.5 *et loc.cit.*

[49] *Queen's Regulations and Admiralty Instructions (1862)* Chapter 35 Art 21.

[50] *Abstract of arrangements respecting registration of births, marriages and deaths in the United Kingdom and other countries of the British Commonwealth of Nations and in the Irish Republic* (HMSO, 1952) p.183.

[51] Consular Marriage Act 1849, 12 & 13 Vic c.68 s.20.

[52] Confirmation of Marriages on HM Ships Act 1879, 42 & 43 Vic c.29.

[53] Marriage Act 1890, 53 & 54 Vic c.47 s.2.

[54] Foreign Marriages Act 1892, 55 & 56 Vic c.23 s.12.

[55] PRO BT 167/151 p.78.

**Merchant Ships**

[56] Farrington, A, *Catalogue of East India Company ships' journals and logs, 1600-1834* (British Library, 1999).

57   Watts, C T and M J Watts, *My Ancestor was a Merchant Seaman*, (2nd edn. Society of Genealogists, 2002).
Smith, K, C T Watts and M J Watts, *Records of Merchant Shipping and Seamen*, PRO Readers' Guide No. 20 (reprint with addendum PRO, 2001).

58   Taylor, P A M, 'Passenger Lists as an Historical Source', *Genealogists' Magazine*, vol.12, no.6 (June 1956) pp.197-200.

59   *Relations in records: A guide to family history sources in the Australian Archives*, (AGPS, Canberra, 1988) pp 6-16.

60   *See* the Concise Guide on their website www.records.nsw.gov.au

61   *Guide to Shipping and Free Passenger Records*, Guide to the State Archives of New South Wales No.17 (2nd edn. 1984) p 37.

62   *Ancestors in Archives: A guide to Family History sources in the official records of South Australia*, (State Records Reference Service Branch, 1991) p.5.

63   Schmidt-Pretoria, Werner, *Deutsche Wanderung nach Süd-Afrika im 19 Jahrhundert* (Berlin: Reimer, 1955).

64   *Family History at National Archives*, (National Archives, Wellington, NZ 1990) pp.26-28 and 31-33.

65   *Guide to Genealogical Research in the National Archives*, (National Archives Trust Fund Board, Washington, D.C., 1983) chapter 2.
Colletta, J P, *They came in ships: A guide to finding your immigrant ancestor's arrival record* (3rd edn. Ancestry, Salt Lake City, 2002).

66   Beine, J, *Finding Passenger Lists & Immigration Records 1820-1940s: arrivals at US ports from Europe* http://home.att.net/~wee-monster/passengers.html

67   *Family History at National Archives*, (National Archives, Wellington, NZ, 1990), pp 61-62.

68   Bromell, A, *Tracing Family History in New Zealand*, (revised and updated edition Wellington, NZ, 1996) p.106.

69   Watts, C T and M J Watts, *My Ancestor was a Merchant Seaman*, (2nd edn. Society of Genealogists, 2002).
Smith, K, C T Watts and M J Watts, *Records of Merchant Shipping and Seamen*, PRO Readers' Guide No. 20 (reprint with addendum PRO, 2001).

[70] *Ships Wrecked or Sunk*, TNA: PRO leaflet: Military Records Information 43.

## Registrar-General of Shipping and Seamen

[71] *Relations in records: A guide to family history sources in the Australian Archives*, (AGPS, Canberra, 1988), p.45

[72] *Relations in records: A guide to family history sources in the Australian Archives*, (AGPS, Canberra, 1988) p.47.

[73] US Coast Guard *Summary of merchant marine personnel casualties, World War II*, (Washington, D.C., 1950).

## Royal Navy

[74] *Ships Wrecked or Sunk*, TNA: PRO leaflet: Military Records Information 43.

[75] Rodger, N A M, *Naval Records for Genealogists,* PRO Handbook No 22 (2nd edn. PRO 1988) p.6.

## Admiralty

[76] Rodger, N A M, *Naval Records for Genealogists,* PRO Handbook No 22 (2nd edn. PRO, 1988) Appendix II.

## Registrars-General of Births, Deaths and Marriages

[77] *Abstract of arrangements respecting registration of births, marriages and deaths in the United Kingdom and other countries of the British Commonwealth of Nations and in the Irish Republic* (HMSO,1952) p.183.

[78] *Abstract of arrangements respecting registration of births, marriages and deaths in the United Kingdom and other countries of the British Commonwealth of Nations and in the Irish Republic* (HMSO,1952) p.183.

[79] *The British Overseas*, Guildhall Library Research Guide 2 (3rd edn. Guildhall Library, 1994).
Bevan, A (ed.), *Tracing your Ancestors in the Public Record Office*, PRO Handbook No 19 (6th edn. PRO, 2002).

[80] Webb, C, *Dates and Calendars for the Genealogist*, (Society of Genealogists 1989).

[81] PRO CO 386/170 f.20 p.19

[82] *GRO War Deaths: Army Officers Indexes 1914-21* records:

| Name | Rank | Unit | Year | Vol. | Page |
|------|------|------|------|------|------|
| KITCHENER | Field | — | 1916 | O.3 | 124 |
| Earl of Khartoum K.G. etc | Marshal | | | | |

[83] *Abstract of arrangements respecting registration of births, marriages and deaths in the United Kingdom and other countries of the British Commonwealth of Nations and in the Irish Republic* (HMSO,1952) p.58.

[84] *Abstract of arrangements respecting registration of births, marriages and deaths in the United Kingdom and other countries of the British Commonwealth of Nations and in the Irish Republic* (HMSO,1952) p.62.

[85] *Abstract of arrangements respecting registration of births, marriages and deaths in the United Kingdom and other countries of the British Commonwealth of Nations and in the Irish Republic* (HMSO,1952).

[86] US Dept. of Health and Human Services, Public Health Service, Centers for Disease Control and Prevention, National Center for Health Statistics *Where to write for Vital Records: Births, deaths, marriages and divorces* (Washington, D.C., 1999).

## Subsidiary Sources

[87] Bevan, A (ed.), *Tracing your Ancestors in the Public Record Office*, PRO Handbook No 19 (6th edn. PRO, 2002).

[88] Watts, C T and M J Watts, *My Ancestor was a Merchant Seaman*, (2nd edn. Society of Genealogists, 2002).

[89] *Trinity House Petitions*, (Society of Genealogists, 1987).

[90] Rodger, N A M, *Naval Records for Genealogists,* PRO Handbook No 22 (2nd edn. PRO, 1988).
Pappalardo, B, *Naval Records for Family Historians*, Readers' Guide No 24 (PRO, 2003)

[91] Thomas, G, *Records of the Royal Marines*, PRO Readers' Guide No. 10, (PRO, 1995).

[92] Hughes, H & L, *Discharged in New Zealand* (New Zealand Society of Genealogists, 1988) and Gavin W Petrie's website at http://freepages.genealogy.rootsweb.com/~shipstonz/auckland1.html

[93] PRO RG 11/4445 f.97 p.12

[94] Society of Genealogists Project Group (transcribers), *St. Anne Limehouse, Middlesex: Monumental Inscriptions* (Summer 1979), stone no 236. A copy is in the Society's library.

[95] Jarvis, S D and D B (compilers) *The Cross of Sacrifice: an alphabetically compiled record of British Officers who died in service of their country identifying where they died and are commemorated.*

vol.1: *Officers who died in the service of British, Indian and East African Regiments and Corps 1914-1919.* (Roberts Medals, Reading, 1993).

vol.2: *Officers who died in the service of the Royal Navy, Royal Navy Reserve, Royal Naval Volunteer Reserve, Royal Marines, Royal Naval Air Service and Royal Air Force 1914-1919.* (Roberts Medals, Reading, 1993).

vol.3: *Officers who died in the service of the British Commonwealth and colonial navies, regiments and corps and air forces 1914-1919.* (Roberts Medals, Reading, 1994).

vol.4: *Non-commissioned officers, men, and women of the United Kingdom, Commonwealth and Empire who died in the service of the Royal Navy, Royal Marines, Royal Naval Air Service, Royal Marines Flying Corp and the Royal Air Force 1914-1921, including the Commonwealth Navies and Air Forces.* (Roberts Medals, Reading, 1996).

vol.5: *The Officers, men and women of the Merchant Navy and Mercantile Fleet Auxiliary 1914-1919,* (Naval & Military Press, c.2001). [This volume also contains a 14 page addendum to Volume 4 that is not available separately].

[96] Tomlinson, B, 'The National Maritime Museum Memorial Index', *Family Tree Magazine*, vol.13 no.10 (August 1997), p.22.

[97] Scott, M, *Prerogative Court of Canterbury Wills and Other Probate Records,* PRO Readers' Guide No. 15 (PRO, 1997).

[98] Camp, A J, 'Births, marriages and deaths at sea', *Family Tree Magazine* vol.17 no.2 (December 2000).pp.9-10

99 Fitch, M, *Index to Testamentary Records in the Archdeaconry Court of London now preserved in the Guildhall Library: Volume 1 (1363)-1649*, (British Record Society, 1979) p.xi

100 Barriskill, D T, *A Guide to the Lloyd's Marine Collection at Guildhall Library* (2nd edn. Guildhall Library, 1994).

101 Watts, C T and M J Watts, *My Ancestor was a Merchant Seaman*, (2nd edn. Society of Genealogists, 2002).

102 Bromell, A, *Tracing Family History in New Zealand*, (revised and updated edition Wellington, NZ, 1996).

103 Manders, F W D (ed.), *Bibliography of British Newspapers: Durham and Northumberland* (British Library, 1982). {Volumes also available on Kent and Wiltshire.}
*Tercentenary Handlist of English and Welsh Newspapers, 1620-1920* (Times, 1920).
Crane, R S and F B Kaye, *Census of British Newspapers 1620-1800*, (1927).

104 Watts, C T and M J Watts, *My Ancestor was a Merchant Seaman*, (2nd edn. Society of Genealogists, 2002).
Smith, K, C T Watts and M J Watts, *Records of Merchant Shipping and Seamen*, PRO Readers' Guide No. 20 (reprint with addendum PRO, 2001).

## Location of Agreements, Crew Lists and Log Books

105 Watts, C T and M J Watts, *My Ancestor was a Merchant Seaman*, (2nd edn. Society of Genealogists, 2002).
Smith, K, C T Watts and M J Watts, *Records of Merchant Shipping and Seamen*, PRO Readers' Guide No. 20 (reprint with addendum PRO, 2001).

106 A Guide to the Crew Agreements and Official Logbooks, 1863-1913, held at the County Record Offices of the British Isles (Maritime History Archive).
Record Offices and Libraries holding Crew Lists and Agreements for 1863-1913, Crew List Index Project (CLIP), Information Sheet No. 3 (2000).
Personal enquires to some record offices.

# INDEX

Principal entries are shown in **bold**. Figures are shown in *Italic*.